BUTTERFLIES ARE NORMAL

for every woman who wants to overcome flutters of anxiety and shine with confidence in her life

RUTH OLIVER

OSTRICH180
PUBLISHING

First published in 2023 by OSTRICH180 Publishing
PO BOX 1133, Toowong, Brisbane 4066, AUSTRALIA
www.ostrich180.com

ISBN: 978-0-6455374-2-0 (Paperback)
ISBN: 978-0-6455374-3-7 (eBook)

NATIONAL LIBRARY OF AUSTRALIA

A catalogue record for this book is available from the National Library of Australia

Text design by JetLaunch
Cover design by JetLaunch
Typeset in Adobe Caslon Pro and NoteWorthy

To Seb and Josh
who will always be my greatest joy

Contents

PART III

APPENDICES

"We shall not cease from exploration, and the end of all our exploring will be to arrive where we started and know the place for the first time."

T.S. Eliot

Authors Note

Welcome, I commend you for picking up this book because it means you are seeking something more from yourself and life. You've chosen to explore, and as an explorer, you will not only improve your own life but the lives of those with whom you come into contact.

This book contains information that I believe, had you learned as a child, practiced as an adolescent, and mastered as an adult, would have made your life easier, happier, and more rewarding. I also believe that within the women who live on this planet, there are enormous amounts of unique talent and capability hidden beneath fear, self-doubt, and lack of confidence. I've always been driven to help people bring out the best in themselves and shine, and throughout my life, I've amassed skills and tools to help people do that. Now, my wish is for you to shine in your life in a way that gives you meaning and pleasure.

The book contains three parts and an appendix. The first three parts will help you understand how your mind works, how you've been conditioned from a young age, and how much of that conditioning can be very unhelpful. I'll walk you through a model called The Four Aspects of Well-Being so you can see clearly how increasing your intellectual, emotional, physical, and spiritual health will help you resolve many of your problems. Not only this you'll understand how enhancing your well-being is the key to unlocking your potential. You will also have an opportunity to explore your own life in more detail concerning The Four Aspects of Well-Being. There are practical exercises for you to do peppered throughout these sections of the book because learning through experience is important. The appendix is where you'll put everything you've learned into action! This last section of the book will teach you practical, simple and effective practices that will enable you to bring the lessons from this book alive in your life so you can enjoy more success and happiness.

As I'm telling you about this practical section of the book, I know that I would be tempted to skip straight to these everyday exercises! You may be thinking the same thing. However, I encourage you to take your time and absorb the information in the first part of the book. Knowledge is power, and there are steps along the way that will greatly enhance your understanding of the benefits you'll gain from the everyday practices.

Ultimately, this book is about taking responsibility for yourself, not because it's been demanded of you by someone else, but because only you can do the inner work necessary to gain a greater level of self-awareness, inner empowerment, capability, and potential, all of which will lead to a more fulfilling life.

Sometimes I wonder what life would be like if it didn't take so long to work this stuff out. Wouldn't it be lovely to go through life without worrying or feeling inadequate or self-conscious? How liberating it would be to feel self-assured and unconcerned with what others think of us. I remember when our boys reached their early teenage years and all the stresses and pains of puberty set in. Spots, growth spurts, needing to wear the right clothes, and be seen in all the right places, which was not with their mother! I often wished that I could put them in a time capsule and catapult them toward their mid-twenties so they could miss all the uncomfortable experiences so many of us go through as teenagers.

But then that's what life is, a journey with lots of phases and stages of good and bad, wanted, and unwanted encounters. We can either grow from these encounters and learn to navigate life with a sense of acceptance and hopefulness or allow them to diminish our light and our life.

My eldest son was born in the British military hospital in Hong Kong in 1990, my husband was an army officer and Hong Kong was our home. Once we left the hospital, I would go with all the other mothers to a local weekly clinic where the nurse would check how our babies were doing. We lived on a very steep hill and trotting down to the clinic in the morning sunshine was a breeze. Coming back up that hill a few hours later, when the heat and humidity had set in, had me leaning almost horizontally into the steep slope pushing the pram with sweat dripping down my back.

When he was only a few weeks old, our son began crying uncontrollably every evening. Like clockwork he would start howling at five o'clock each night, his face getting redder and his little body writhing as he became more and more distressed. Most people associate Hong Kong with the hustle and bustle of a big city, but we lived on the eighth floor of an apartment block in the New Territories surrounded by countryside. I would pace around our apartment and out onto the balcony rocking my baby in my arms, not knowing what to do while his screams echoed across the countryside. It was hard to believe such a loud painful cry could come from something so tiny.

On one of my weekly trips down the hill to see the nurse, I mentioned this distressing problem. "It'll pass, it's probably colic. It's just a stage he's going through," she said, giving me a bottle of herbal tonic called gripe water. Sure enough, a few weeks later it passed, and the crying stopped. There were many things I asked her about as my tiny baby rapidly changed over those first six months, and often her advice was, "Don't worry, it'll pass." I'm grateful I met that lovely nurse all those years ago because her words have been a comfort to me all my life; not only to know that the phases and stages my children go through will pass but also the stages of whatever pain, discomfort, or resistance I'm feeling will also pass. I've considered getting "*This too shall pass*," tattooed on the inside of my wrist, as a reminder of this wisdom.

It's said that this phrase was originally born from an eastern monarch who charged his wise men to write a sentence that will be true and appropriate at all times. I think they did a good job. It's not only timeless, and true, it's very reassuring, because, as I've learned throughout my life, colic is just the beginning. We go through constant stages and changes in our lives; much of it is welcome, but often it's unwanted and causes upset, trauma and anxiety. As I've travelled through the stages and challenges of my life, I've been incredibly fortunate to have had wise mentors and teachers who have shown me there is inner work to be done if we are to move through these difficulties more easily.

My aim in writing this book is to help you understand your inner world of thoughts, beliefs, and emotions that are a natural consequence of engaging in life. And to give you some tools and skills to help you manage them, so you can navigate the challenges of life with as much ease, clarity, and control as possible. Why? Because you have unique and important talents that the world needs and having the ability to face challenges with composure and confidence will help you bring these talents to the world.

We've all experienced the flutter of nervous butterflies in the tummy, and at times gnawing feelings of panic and anxiety, that can lead us to believe there's something wrong with us. Well, I aim to help you see that as you navigate the inevitable challenges in your life - butterflies are normal. Furthermore, you'll realise that feeling anxious and worried at times is a shared human experience that's perfectly natural. Befriending those butterflies is what will enable you to set them free, so you can unlock your unique potential and shine in your life.

So, let's begin the process of understanding how we get stuck. Are you ready?

PART I

Chapter 1
The P-word

"Oh no, my dad's going to kill me!" moaned my friend, sitting next to me on the school bus. We'd been given our school reports and as was our ritual at this time of year, we were carefully prising open the slim brown envelope to read the contents and prepare ourselves for the onslaught that would inevitably come if they were bad. This was the '70s, in today's technological world it's hard to believe we were handed our reports to dutifully deliver to our parents.

Each teacher would write their report on a slim piece of thin paper. There was a printed line at the top of the slip where the teacher filled in the subject and date. At the bottom of the page was another line for the teacher's signature, then some space in the middle for comments. But the bit our eyes darted to before we read any of the comments was the line opposite the signature on which the dreaded grade was written. Somewhere between A and D, plus or minus. It either made your heart sing – or sink.

The report slips were placed behind a red card cover with our name and school grade on the front. Neatly collated, they were then stapled in the top left-hand corner. I knew before I read the subject heading who had written the report by the familiar and always neat handwriting of each teacher. The brown envelopes in which they were placed were smooth but not very robust, which made them hard to open without ripping the paper.

I'd sit at the back of the bus turning each tissue-thin page of my report, ever hopeful of some recognition or praise. It rarely seemed to come. Year after year the resounding message was "Ruth isn't reaching her potential in this subject." "Ruth has way more potential than she is demonstrating." There were some encouraging comments and good grades, but they were drowned out by this problem I seemed to have of "not reaching my potential." The word leaped off the page and made me feel incapable and deflated as year after year I failed at reaching this elusive state.

In my young mind, I thought that potential was a goal or a destination I would finally realise. To me, this goal seemed to be somewhere in the future when I would have A+ written on every corner of my report slips and glowing comments from all my teachers. Everyone would be happy with me, and I'd finally be recognised and rewarded once I achieved my potential. But there seemed to be nothing but dissatisfaction and disappointment emanating from that neat handwriting. I gave myself little to no credit for the things I was achieving, and the value placed on my academic accomplishments seemed to be far more important than anything else. Surely once I had everyone's approval, I'd feel better.

As well as challenging times, there will also be times you remember from your childhood when you felt fully alive without a care in the world, a free, innocent spirit unencumbered by life. They might have been fleeting, rare moments, or perhaps they happened often. You may have experienced feeling fearless and unstoppable, or perhaps very peaceful, calm, and trusting. These moments happened when you were engaged in a certain activity or were in a memorable place or with a special person. Maybe they were moments of silence when you were in nature and loved the feeling of the sun on your face and the sound of the birds. Or times of adventure and excitement, like jumping into the cold ocean or feeling somewhat out of control as you raced downhill on your bike with the wind in your hair. Or perhaps you would get lost in moments of cuddling your soft, affectionate dog or staring at the sky. These moments may be vague now, but if you cast your mind back, there will be moments like this you remember from when you were a child. Moments of deep simplicity and knowing when you felt totally at one with yourself and your world, with no hang-ups, no agenda, no worries or anxieties. You were pure potential with unhindered life force flowing through you.

What was your moment? Where were you? What's your childhood memory of feeling totally at one with yourself and your world, peaceful, happy, content, and trusting of life?

For me, it was always when we were on our regular walking holidays in the Lake District in North West England. As you can imagine, a walking holiday for a child wasn't always the most appealing of adventures. But I enjoyed these holidays a lot because we went with other families and friends and had great fun. Our parents would map out long walks and I loved being outside in nature, surrounded by the stunning mountains, lakes and rivers, even when it meant traipsing up a mossy hillside in the pouring rain.

Often while on these long walks in the mountains I would hang back from the group. I'd wait until everyone was out of sight, either around a corner or over the brow of a craggy hill, until I was alone. If you saw a young child alone on the side of a hill you'd probably rush to her aid. But in those moments of stillness and silence, completely alone without another human being in sight, I was never happier. I was unafraid. I felt protected and very peaceful.

As the voices of my family and friends faded away and I was left with the wind on my face, the smell of the earth, and the birds for company, I hoped no one would come along to break that moment. The farther away my family and friends got and the more isolated I became, the more content and peaceful I felt. I thought nothing could ever beat being in this place; it felt like home as if I were remembering a state of being that was completely natural and very alluring.

What I now realise is that these innocent moments we experience as children reveal the part of us that is fearless, trusting, inspired potential, later lost to us in adulthood. For me, they were fleeting moments, and the blissful feeling was deeply powerful but short-lived, as someone would come running back to get me. "Hurry up, come on, catch up." And I'd be pulled out of this delightful state.

What was your moment? As you cast your mind back, just let it come to you. What were you doing when you experienced as a child the pure bliss of simply being, with no limits, no restrictions, feeling safe and trusting in life? Let me tell you why I call those times my onion bulb moments.

Chapter 2
Onions

I want you to visualise an onion. I like those dark purple onions, but whatever kind of onion appeals to you, see it in your mind's eye. Imagine the onion sitting on your kitchen bench and notice how the outer dry skin can be opened up revealing a shiny new layer underneath. Of course, underneath that first shiny layer, there are many more layers to this onion. Now imagine cutting your onion in half. As the two halves open, you'll see there are layers and layers to this onion all perfectly formed and tightly packed together. Now look into the centre of that onion, right in the middle of all those outer layers, you'll see that there's a tiny little bulb. You may have cut it in half when you sliced through your onion, but it's there, right in the middle, a shiny perfect bulb, protected by all the outer layers.

Of course, you know without having to cut open an onion that there are layers and layers of flesh around the bulb, one on top of the other. I like to use the analogy of the onion to describe how we also have layers and layers of protection around us. These are layers of thoughts, emotions, beliefs, and habits that we have established based on our conditioning and experience of life, put in place to help us feel protected.

By the end of this book, you'll understand how those layers were formed and how some of them are no longer serving you, and even keeping you stuck in some areas of your life. You'll see how easy it is to gently peel them away and become re-acquainted with that part of yourself you knew as a child, unencumbered by these layers of protection. You'll see how allowing these shields to drop away is liberating, enlightening, and necessary for you to know your real potential.

Peeling an onion reminds me of the layers of history, memories, and emotions in which we wrap ourselves as we grow up, and that under all those layers we are pure potential, with a capacity to live life without the restrictions of our conditioning. And then of course I begin to question, what happened to that potential? Where did it go, and why is this life journey full of so many obstacles? Why is it so challenging at times, even for people like me who've had a relatively easy life and been bought up by wonderful loving parents who take their children on wet, windy walking holidays!

Well, that's what we're going to discover together. How did all those layers of conditioning end up suppressing our potential? And, how come we can't get to that potential without peeling them away? How did it become so difficult to access that part of ourselves we knew in those simple moments of childhood when we were bold, trusting, and uninhibited?

Let's go back again to when you were a child or teenager. I want you to pick an event or situation that made you shrink or shy away. It doesn't need to be something awful. I remember vividly one of my teachers shouting down the school hallway in front of all my friends that I'd failed my biology exam, adding that my sister would never have done such a thing. Perhaps you also failed exams, did something you're ashamed of, didn't make the sports team, or felt ostracised at school. What was it for you?

If you think back to your own life experiences, you'll see that at times you've been open to your potential and at other times closed and resistant to the things you encounter. I'm sure you can recall times when you've been willing, confident, and excited about something that's on your horizon, trusting that you're going to enjoy the process and keen to see what you're capable of; even though it may have been a little scary. And at other times I'm sure you can remember feeling closed, uneasy, resistant, and even afraid of taking the next step. Our ability to be willing and open to life or our tendency to close to the opportunities that come our way is informed and influenced by our past experiences.

The experience of being singled out and compared unfavourably to my sister, by someone in a position of authority, in front of all my friends, was in my teenage mind embarrassing and humiliating. It represents a typical moment when we are likely to tell ourselves we do not want to have that experience again. So, to feel safe, respected, and accepted we unconsciously put on some armour, a layer of protection, and rework our behaviour. Can you sense how easy it is for a young unaware mind to compute that, if we don't want to be embarrassed again, we need to become something different? Maybe we decide that being a perfectionist will resolve that unwanted attention? Or we think becoming the cool kid will counterbalance the feelings of humiliation. This is a natural process that we go through as we grow up, separating ourselves from our true nature, which is another way of saying pure potential, by creating identities that we believe will support us. I think I made a pact with myself at that moment in the crowded school corridor, that I would find something else to be recognised for, and as it wasn't academics, sport was going to be my saviour. Without the wisdom and maturity to turn these kinds of experiences into positive, learning opportunities, we file them away in our unconscious mind, in the "not to be repeated file," and to ensure that happens we close off a piece of ourselves and shy away from that part of our life.

Why do we do this? Simply because we don't want to experience pain or fear. Feeling diminished as a child and not possessing the wisdom or life skills to remain open in the face of our hurt and pain, will result in an unconscious decision to alter our beliefs and behaviour to restore feelings of safety. We do this by either devaluing or inflating ourselves, and in doing so our potential becomes more and more inhibited. As we draw these layers of protection around us, we accept that it's normal to feel this way.

Who knows, maybe I could have been a pioneering biologist and at that moment my career was ruined! No, I was never going to be a scientist, but this experience penetrated my being as a message that rendered me useless at that moment and informed my sense of self-worth. And being humiliated as a teenager in front of your friends is a wound you're going to put a very tight bandage on. And so, as life goes on, we become aware that we are being judged, criticised, examined, made wrong, or hurt and we begin drawing those layers of protection tightly around us. "But protection is good," I hear you say, "I don't want to feel hurt or upset, so of course I'm going to protect myself!" Yes, of course you are, but there's a better way to do it. With a deeper understanding of your true nature and a change of focus you can feel safe and capable despite the negative experiences that come your way, and without diminishing your potential.

Chapter 3
The Narrow Road

Let's look at it another way. Here's where I get you to visualise again. Imagine that you're standing on a road or track. It's empty with no traffic, it looks appealing, and you feel incredibly happy to be here. Now, make sure you get this visualisation clear because we'll be coming back to this road later. The road has bushes and trees along its edges, there's no one else on it, just you, standing in the middle. You begin to walk down the road, feeling calm and happy. The sun's shining, the birds are singing, and you know that when you reach the end of this road, you'll have enormous success and enjoy a sense of happiness and contentment as you've never felt before. You're excited as you eagerly keep walking because you're keen to unlock the potential that awaits you at the end of this road. Now, imagine that as you continue to walk, full of enthusiasm, suddenly someone jumps out of the bushes. They're waving a big stick, shouting and threatening you, and you cower down feeling shocked and confused. Once the danger passes, you're keen to continue walking but you're feeling a little shaky and tentative now, this welcoming and exciting journey is not as appealing as it first seemed. But you're spurred on anyway, knowing that at the end of this road you're going to experience enormous happiness and success.

You keep walking, cautiously at first then after a while you begin to relax, feeling more confident and telling yourself everything will be all right. Just as you're getting back into your stride another person jumps out at you, even more angry and aggressive than the last. Your whole system is jolted by this sudden assault on your senses, and you jump back and try to protect yourself. This time it takes a while for your heart rate to come down and you begin to question your ability to cope, but eventually, you calm yourself down and get back into your stride. Still feeling shaky, and not enjoying your walk any longer you're relieved to come to a fork in the road and an opportunity to travel a much narrower track. It looks easier to navigate, there's no foliage for scary people to jump out of and you can see clearly in every direction. As you turn down this easier track you breathe a sigh of relief, happy to be in your comfort zone again. But it's very clear to you that this new track doesn't hold the excitement, happiness, or success that was at the end of the other one; in fact, it looks pretty boring, and you know instantly that you're not going to experience the love of life that you would on the big open road. But hey, you convince yourself that you'll be content with this more ordinary limited experience and less success; it'll be for the best, who wants to keep having all those scary incidents? You settle back into a comfortable stride, convincing yourself that taking this safe and easy route is the better choice. Excitement, happiness, and potential ... who cares about that right now? You just want to feel safe. But as you glance down the track ahead you can see a shadow in the distance. You can't quite make out what it is, but it doesn't look very welcoming. Your pace slows almost to a stop as you try to determine what's standing in your way. Now you wonder whether it's worth continuing at all. Is it safe, is what awaits you going to be another awful experience? Maybe it's best to just stay put and not move at all.

To one degree or another, we are always journeying on the road towards our potential. It may not seem that way sometimes, but as human beings, we are constantly striving to improve, we can't help ourselves. We are hard-wired to try and succeed. Therefore, we are continually aiming for our dreams and desires, whether they be to eat more healthily, improve our relationships, save for a holiday, get a promotion, get fit, or get out of bed. We are constantly endeavouring to improve and are innately programmed to move forward and develop in big and small ways.

Our effort to fulfill our potential starts the moment we're born, and as we journey down the road of life many perceived obstacles will jump out at us or block our pathway, like my schoolteacher. These obstacles and shocks will often cause us to bring up a layer of protection just like the ones around the onion bulb. The wide-open road of possibility, that we were excited to venture down when we were born, becomes a tiny, curtailed path that leads to somewhere we convince ourselves we're vaguely happy with. We're not really, but at least we feel safe, and life is relatively easy and pain-free.

The problem, and the gift, is that your road holds the key to your happiness, no matter what is achieved or gained along the way. To be able to stride down the wide-open road of life as a confident, capable, and receptive woman, gracefully weaving in and out of obstacles, and navigating the sinister shadows ahead, is how we reach our potential and feel happy and successful.

Do you remember that childhood moment, the one where you felt unstoppable, trusting, powerful, and in love with life? That's what's down your road. It's not the material stuff we're after, although that's a nice perk along the way; it's a feeling we're searching for. The feeling of inspiration, purpose, life force and potential is what we're after; and the obstacles on our road will stop us in our tracks if we're not taught how to navigate them.

We don't remember those moments of pure potential we had as children because we were gaining something material, we remember those moments because of the feelings we experienced. The inner essence of you doesn't seek a new pair of shoes, more money, or a six-week holiday, nice as those things may be. What you seek is the feeling those things give you. What you seek above anything else is to feel. So, what is it that you want to feel? Coming up is your first exercise – Tuning into Feeling.

Let's get silent and ask some questions and see if we can uncover the truth of what it is that you wish to feel. Read the first question, then close your eyes and sit in silence for a few moments, let the answer to the question emerge from what I call your "wise brain." In other words, don't analyse it or think about it too hard. Just plant the question and let the answer come to you. Then do the same with the second and third questions.

Exercise 1 – Tuning into Feeling

Find a quiet place to sit and have a pen and your notebook ready. After each question close your eyes – when you have your answer write it down in your notebook.

1) If you were to wake up in the morning feeling satisfied with yourself, your life, and your purpose for being here, what would you be feeling?

Try not to let your mind draw you to concrete achievements; instead, make a list of adjectives that describe how you'd feel, for example – I'd feel confident, excited, content, and optimistic.

Go ahead and identify your top three.

2) Imagine you're going about your life, you're on track with your desires, you have a sense of vision and purpose and you're loving life. Then an enormous challenge comes along and throws your life into turmoil.

   How would you like to feel as you tackle this challenge?

Again, this is not a list of things you would do, but a list of words describing how you would like to feel as you address this problem. For example - I'd want to feel capable, composed, and optimistic. How about you? Close your eyes and let the feelings come to you.

3) Now imagine your day is coming to an end. It's been a full and successful day and you've been engaged with the things that are most important to you. How would you like to feel at the end of your day?

Would it be satisfied, enlightened, challenged, or calm, content, and slightly chuffed? Or something completely different. Close your eyes and pick your top three end-of-day feelings.

My question to you is this: Would you rather push through life feeling stressed, tired, and incomplete, believing the short-term fix of a holiday is the answer to your problems? Or would you rather have reliable positive, uplifting feelings permeate your body and mind as you travel down the road to greater contentment and success?

Are you beginning to see how you may have narrowed your wide-open road, that used to hold all possibilities, down to a narrow path of "make do" and "hope for the best?"

So, how does this happen? How is it that we get to a stage in our lives where we've shelved our dreams and desires and are simply getting by and putting up with less than we hoped for? Whether you want to be a better parent, a better co-worker, own a cake shop, be healthier, happier, be a great leader or save the planet, why did you narrow your sights and put your potential on the back burner? Now, I want to say at this point that this book is not only for women who have what society would perceive as big dreams. So, if you're thinking that this book isn't for you because you don't have anything noteworthy that you're desiring in life, let me point out that you're doing it again. Allowing your past to determine your future, putting another layer of armour on, and narrowing your path.

Whether your dream is to get out of bed or end world poverty, your potential matters. It's needed to achieve whatever it is that will bring a sense of meaning to your life and positive change to the world. Whether you wish to illuminate your life or someone else's, show yourself more love, or love someone else more, build a community service, or a huge corporation, tidy up your back yard or save the planet; there are no doubt intellectual, emotional, physical, or spiritual blocks that are keeping you on a narrow and limited path of unfulfilled dreams.

What you'll learn from this book are not motivational techniques to boost you up and push you on. Instead, it will help you do the inner work necessary to navigate life as a more confident, calm, resilient, and loving woman. A woman who feels in control and can break free of unhelpful conditioned habits and holding patterns. Your dreams are never too small or insignificant to work toward, your valuable life is full of promise and potential, and it's these qualities that will enable you to boldly stride down your path. This is where real motivation comes from.

Now it's time to lengthen your stride, lighten your step, and hold your face to the sun. It's time to prepare for the obstacles ahead, because there will always be obstacles, and clear the ones from your past that are still lurking in the undergrowth and holding you back.

Let's summarise before we move on. You were born with unadulterated potential. As you began your journey through life you had moments as a child when you experienced your potential as confidence, determination, trust, and unbridled joy. But, as you grew into a teenager and then a young adult you tried to stay open and excited about your journey, but things got in the way. The challenging situations you faced often left you feeling less than confident. People's harsh words diminished your sense of self-worth, hurtful actions from others ate away at your self-esteem. In a bid to protect yourself and navigate your life journey in a more comfortable way you either dimmed your light, berated, and negated yourself, or puffed yourself up and put on a front. Either one made life feel easier and less confrontational in the short term, but at the same time diminished your long-term potential. These negative events made you fear the road ahead and rather than stride down it with confidence and excitement you began to creep forward with uncertainty, often with an inner voice of doubt and criticism as your companion. No longer are you in touch with that child who knew no bounds and felt trusting of life. You became an adult, with a dim and distant memory of what your true unbridled potential used to be.

Okay, that's the gloom and doom over with. My point here is that to one degree or another we are all affected by our experiences in life, for good or bad. They will either become a layer of protection and fear or liberate us to another level of understanding and capability. The good news is that the incidents that worried and confused you as you ventured down your road of life were not what stopped you in your tracks. Just as challenging events were not what caused you to change your course. It was the stories you told yourself about those events that became embedded as negative mind chatter and informed your choices. Any fall-out that occurred in my life because my teacher chose a crowded corridor full of my friends to announce I'd failed my exam was not her fault. The fall-out occurred because of the story I chose to construct about myself due to that incident. My mind chatter was my undoing. No one can diminish your sense of self-worth with their actions alone; the pain is caused not by the event, but by the beliefs we have about it. I'm not condoning unhelpful or bad behaviour, but to be able to grow and thrive we must take responsibility for, and control, our thoughts, and beliefs.

I wish everyone was taught this stuff in primary school. Your mind is a magnificent tool that can be used to uplift and move you forward in a positive direction. It's not a deep, dark place waiting to trip you up, but it will if you don't keep a check on the stories it's telling you.

Chapter 4
A Change of Story

First, I want to tell you a little about why I'm writing this book. I'm a well-being coach and bring together my experience as a yoga and meditation teacher, thought field therapy practitioner, and self-esteem coach to help women live happier and more successful lives. When you ignore your intellectual, emotional, physical, or spiritual well-being you do so at a huge cost to your happiness and tragically your health. Women can easily fall victim to this pattern of neglect as they put their needs aside to juggle multiple roles and responsibilities. I work with women who want to stop living with anxiety, self-doubt, stress, or lack of confidence and are ready to take responsibility for their well-being and control the way they feel. Through education, self-inquiry, meditation, and other practices, I help my clients proactively stay on an upward spiral of well-being, from where they can unlock their potential and fully enjoy life.

As I write this book, I hope it will offer you encouragement and inspiration, wherever you happen to be on your life journey. Perhaps you are an old hand at meditation and self-reflection and it will help to encourage you. Or maybe you're new to the world of personal development. Maybe you've dabbled in yoga, but when you heard the teacher use the classical Indian language of Sanskrit to describe the next posture you thought they were about to order a takeaway! You may have been on a retreat or ventured to a local meditation class that enabled you to relax more deeply than you ever have before. Somewhere along the line you've realised there's more value to be had from examining your inner world, but you're not sure what it is. Or you may have come by the Western route and had some experience with a therapist or psychologist that you found useful. It was good to get help, and now you're keen to take control of your life independently. Something within you instinctively understands that you have the answers to your problems and that you can help yourself move through your self-doubt and inner demons. And you can. Perhaps you're not quite sure where to start and how to keep the momentum of positive change going.

Here's some food for thought; this piece of information alone, if taken on board and observed in your own life will help you enormously. Here it is: All negative emotions stem from fear. Let me say that again: All negative emotions stem from fear. From her decades of work, the highly acclaimed psychiatrist Elisabeth Kübler-Ross observed that there are only two fundamental emotions, fear and love, and all other emotions stem from these two. In the East, Buddhist philosophy identifies the same dichotomy. Realising that they are opposites and cannot be felt at the same time and that all other emotions can be traced back to these two, helps us understand ourselves at a much deeper level.

Any emotion we feel that is challenging or unhelpful stems from fear. Think about it. When you're angry with your children you're afraid of something, perhaps afraid for them, or afraid you're failing or being judged as a parent. When things aren't going well at work you may find yourself snapping at your co-workers because you fear being thought of as incapable. The emotion you feel as you argue with your partner may be resentment, but the resentment stems from fear. Understanding the origin of our emotions is the first step towards controlling them, rather than allowing them to control us.

Let's get back on our road, the one we were on at the beginning before it started to get narrow and fearful. Imagine yourself back on that road now, see it stretching before you like a ribbon of excitement and anticipation, reaching onto the horizon. We begin our journey on that road as we come into the world from the warm comfort of our mother's womb. Sometimes there may be things that impact our sense of well-being immediately, such as a long problematic birth. Some children are born to drug-addicted mothers, which of course is going to impact a child's first experience of their world significantly. So, here we are, tiny babies, some who've had a smooth entry into the world in a caring, loving, environment; others who have had a more traumatic start to life. But we've arrived from the warm, dim, effortless cocoon of our mother's womb and into the cold bright lights of the world in which we are now going to live. Hundreds of new experiences are assaulting our senses as soon as we enter the world.

But let's skip forward a few months. By six to eight months we've developed the ability to determine what's outside the norm. Once our memory is developed, we recognise things that are familiar and unfamiliar to us, and we develop the capacity to be afraid when separated from what's recognisable. Babies often get upset when handed to a stranger, because they are aware that this person is not known to them and they feel fearful. Gradually, we become acclimatised, but only a few months into life we are already experiencing things we don't enjoy that put us on high alert. But our sense of trust is strong, people are good, we get fed, picked up, and cuddled. What's to worry about? Everything is okay. Remember that shiny bulb inside the onion? Well, that was you, trusting, hopeful, and full of potential.

Now you're trying to walk and talk, and life begins to get exciting. You begin to push yourself up to standing and express yourself and there's a whole new view of life from this angle. Can you imagine how exciting this would be for a toddler? How liberating it would be to be able to adjust yourself, so you have a good vantage point, move around the room, and let your voice be heard.

Your senses are now being stimulated in a way they've never been before, and you love this new exploration into life. Toddlers eat mud, mash their food in between their little fingers or splash in puddles without any concern for getting wet. Everything is an experience and something new to investigate. They don't care if they get dirty or cold, they're just here to enjoy the experience. If you have children of your own, you'll know what I mean. You may even be going through this toddler stage with your children right now. These things they do are fun, for a while, then as a mother we get the urge to clean all the mess up. Little hands pressing into the dirt and squeezing the wet mud between their fingers is something we can see they're enjoying, but as the mud gets all over their coat, a parent will want to clean that mess up! It's great fun to let them splash in the puddles if they don't get too wet, at which point we'll whisk them inside and put some dry clothes on them.

In my home country of England where even in summer it can be cool, children will have all the fun in the world in the cold ocean. They love splashing in the icy waves and running in and out of the grey water as if their bodies were completely resistant to temperature. They're having so much fun they don't even feel the cold. As parents, we've forgotten that feeling of being absorbed in the moment with an unrestrained enjoyment of life. So, we let them stay in the cold water just long enough to give them the freedom that any good earth mother would, then we wrap them up in an enormous beach towel and get them dried and clothed, lest they catch pneumonia.

We begin early in life to process our experiences and try to make sense of them. But without the wisdom to understand why these things are happening, we process them the only way we know how. When we don't understand why we've been hastily pulled away from an activity that we're happily engrossed in, we may form the opinion that what we enjoy isn't important. When we don't care about being warm and dry and we're told to stop enjoying splashing in cold water, we may form a belief that having fun isn't allowed. We begin to experience being told how to behave, we're told off, punished, even shouted at, and sadly for some, psychologically and physically abused. We see things on television we don't understand and feel doubt and confusion. And of course, these days social media will add another layer of complexity to this process. We quickly begin to realise that there are things we like and things we don't like. Things we want and things we don't want. Things that make us comfortable and happy, and things that make us uncomfortable and unhappy. And now we are also beginning to realise that when we make our wants and needs known, they are not always well-received.

Cast your mind back, to those dim distant memories of temper tantrums; hopefully, you're not still having them in quite the same way. Defiant sit-ins at the dining-room table refusing to eat your vegetables, refusing to put your shoes on, or do your homework. My elder son spent much of his second year in the world having temper tantrums. These outbursts would build slowly as he realised things were not as he wanted them to be. Gradually he'd become enraged, with tears streaming down his screwed-up face, his knees would buckle underneath him, and he'd sink to the floor, lost in a world of frustration. Unfortunately, the lovely nurse who took care of him when he was born was no longer my trusted advisor, but her words rang in my ears. As my son dropped through my arms like a slippery eel, completely inconsolable, I'd hear her words. As people walked past me in the supermarket with my hysterical child flailing on the floor, I'd tell myself "it will pass." In the playground, on the street, in the car, whenever these outbursts occurred my mantra became, "this, too shall pass." Thankfully, it did, in fact, he's now such a calm and composed young man, I often wonder whether he got all his rage out early in life and simply has none left!

As we venture into our early childhood, we have already begun to distrust ourselves, others, and the world around us, and we find it difficult to understand exactly what is troubling us. Then we go to school and a whole new set of experiences are upon us. So, we begin the process of discerning how to navigate the world in a way that makes us feel comfortable, and how to best avoid experiencing feelings and emotions that make us uncomfortable.

Think back to your best memory of primary school. Where were you, what were you doing, and who were you with? My best experience was being in the classroom with my favourite teacher, Mrs. Southgate. I was eight when Mrs. Southgate came into my life, and I loved her. I particularly remember a project we did on famous authors and poets. For some reason, I chose to study William Shakespeare, quite impressive for an eight-year-old! As was her way, Mrs. Southgate gave us the freedom to present our projects however we wanted to. Some of my classmates wrote about their author, others made clay models or painted pictures to tell the story of their famous person. Mrs. Southgate was very into art, which was right up my alley. On this occasion, I chose to make an enormous picture of William out of tiny screwed-up balls of tissue paper. I sketched his oval face and receding hairline with a big white Elizabethan ruffle around his neck. As each tiny ball was glued into position, the dye from the tissue paper stained my fingers, and as more and more coloured tissue balls were put into place the picture emerged.

I kept that picture for years, probably even a decade. Not because I was a huge fan of William Shakespeare, and not because of the enormous attention to detail that had gone into this work of art. I'm quite sure I kept that picture because the experience of making it was so memorable. I was expressing myself exactly as I wanted to, enjoying the unfolding of my endeavours and feeling validated and capable. I felt thrilled and energised by the process, as I'm sure many of the other children did. Not because we were told how wonderful we were or given a prize for our hard work, but because we were given the time and freedom to flourish in our own way.

The feelings we experience as we grow up inform us about ourselves and the world. It's the felt sense of the experiences we have that determine our future behaviour. Often, we'll feel safe, so we'll be bold and grow from our adventures; at other times we feel afraid, so we shut down and diminish our light.

Now skip to your teenage years. Oh boy, will there be some fodder to work with here. Even if you were the perfect student and never argued with your parents or siblings, something pushed your buttons during this period of your life. Hormones are raging, sexual preferences are becoming clear, peer pressure is at an all-time high, attractions are being formed, a whole new world is opening. And of course, the first real academic pressures of life begin. Being tested, graded high or low, seen as good or bad, being pitched against each other, oh joy!

Cast your mind back now to your favourite teacher at high school. Mine I can think of instantly. Mr. Skelton, RIP. Mr. Skelton was my history and physical education teacher. My mother finds it entertaining to get our school reports out periodically when my sisters and I are home together. We're all in our 50's but I guess you never stop being a mother. As I look through these reports, it's clear that the only time I ever got an A+ in history, or in any subject for that matter, was in grade nine, when Mr. Skelton was my teacher. It's a testimony to what a fabulous teacher he was. Was it because he ruled us with a fist of iron? No. Did he dole out detentions left right and centre? No. Did he mollycoddle us and tell us how wonderful we were? No. He made his students feel excited about the subject they were learning and inspired us to work hard. His classes were fun and interesting, we respected him and in return, he treated us as though we were the most important people in his life. Do you hear that word "feel" again? The reason people excelled in Mr. Skelton's class and loved him as a teacher was because he inspired us to achieve, and that made us feel good about ourselves.

One of the high grades I achieved was for a project on the War of the Roses, a series of English civil wars fought between the Houses of Lancaster and York for control of the throne of England. The wars were named many years later from the badges of the contending Houses, the White Rose of York, and the Red Rose of Lancaster. I can even see in my mind's eye the picture of a white and red rose that I drew on the cover of my project. But why decades later would I remember these two teachers and projects from my school days? I believe it's because both these people enabled me to experience my full potential at that time. These teachers inspired me and many other pupils to do our best, not because we needed to impress them or they demanded that we work hard, but because they had the rare knack of drawing more ability from us than we knew we had. They enabled us to believe in ourselves and thrive.

The memory of that feeling stays with us forever. Why? Because it reminds us how we are meant to be living, like the trusting, curious, excited bulb of potential we were born as. I asked my friends about their memories of favourite teachers and their answers were like mine, their recollections are filled with descriptions of how they felt empowered when in this person's presence. We're lucky if we have a Mrs. Southgate or a Mr. Skelton in our lives. Empowering experiences in childhood instill in us a sense of self-worth that contributes enormously to our confidence and ongoing ability to believe in ourselves and be successful. These experiences propel us on what I call an upward spiral of potential.

But ultimately, it's up to us to foster that feeling of value and worthiness within ourselves. Staying on an upward spiral of well-being can be helped by the people in our lives; equally, some experiences will take us on a downward spiral of despair. It's not useful or reliable to depend on others to reinforce our sense of wholeness or feelings of success. We must clear the inner blocks and beliefs that stand in the way of our success and develop an inner dialogue that's encouraging and inspiring. It's an inside job we must learn to do for ourselves.

We can remember the best of the best and the worst of the worst from our past, because of the feelings these experiences evoked. But how do these experiences seep into our system and determine the level of vigour and confidence with which we travel down life's road? That's what we're going to discover.

Chapter 5
Your Amazing Mind

Let's talk a bit about this thing we have called the mind. What is it made of? Where exactly is it? Can you locate it in your body? It is widely accepted that the mind is separated into what's called the "conscious" and the "unconscious" mind. The conscious mind is a data processor or thinking mind, but it has limited processing capacity, no memory, and can only handle a few tasks at a time. When the conscious mind is active it is totally focused and fully present. You are using your conscious mind now as you read and take in this information. The unconscious mind is where the biography of our life is stored. It holds your memories, emotions, beliefs, and habits and it operates on autopilot. In other words, the information held in the unconscious mind will surface randomly at any time, rather than by deliberate request. So, here's something for you to ponder. How much of your mind do you think is engaged with conscious activity, and how much is unconscious? What percentage of your decisions, emotions, actions, or behaviours are you fully conscious of and focus on with one hundred percent present moment attention? And what percentage of your mind is on autopilot, engaged in generating thoughts, beliefs, habits, and memories arbitrarily? You're going to be surprised!

Many cognitive neuroscientists have conducted studies revealing that only 3% of our cognitive activities are conscious, and the remaining 97% are generated unconsciously. You might ask, what's the problem with that? Well, apart from the fact that it means we are missing out on fully experiencing some very precious moments of our lives, unfortunately, we humans are often geared toward negativity. Research shows that we have thousands of thoughts every day. Up to 95% of these thoughts are the same repetitive ones we had the day before and up to 80% have a negative quality to them.

Think of your unconscious mind like a backpack. As you travel down the road of life you always carry this backpack with you, and in it, you store away all the experiences you encounter along the way. Remember, the unconscious mind is where the biography of your life is stored. As a very young child, you may have encountered someone being angry and aggressive towards you, and the experience left you feeling upset and confused. You packed that experience away in your backpack. Then you experienced the feeling of sadness and loss and you put that one away in your backpack, too. You suffered embarrassment, shame, guilt, and fear. All these memories and feelings are stored away in that pack. Of course, the joyful, exciting, and exhilarating experiences you've had are also in the backpack. So, you're on your way, growing up and moving down the road of life, not quite sure what the journey holds, already carrying quite a heavy load on your back and doing the best you can. This load goes everywhere with you. Even when you rest you never take that backpack off.

Every experience we have in life is being monitored by this amazing thing we all have called a mind. When I felt empowered in my history class, my mind and body took in that experience and filed it away as one to be remembered and emulated. On the other hand, humiliation, embarrassment, hurt, and pain are also stored away in the mind-body system. These memories will alert us when it looks like we may be in danger of facing unpleasant emotions again.

A joy, a challenge, a delight, a disaster, the events of our life keep coming and we store the memories, feelings, and emotions deep within our mind-body system. Sometimes we're confident and stride with more purpose down the road of life, at other times the stories we've stored in our unconscious mind remind us to keep our pace slow and constrained. Hopefully, we develop some awareness and self-compassion and can release some of the negative impacts these memories have on us. Mostly what happens is we bottle up these memories and feelings, and as we reinforce them over time they become beliefs we have about ourselves that inform our sense of self-esteem and identity. But, because we are action-orientated beings, and are not taught to understand where our unhelpful thoughts and emotions come from, we battle on. Our inner critic rings loudly in our ears leading to feelings of self-doubt, anxiety, and confusion. But we forge on down the road of life, trying on new identities to fit in and feel happier.

If you look back, you can probably recognise some of the identities you adopted at different stages in your life; it's inevitable that as we're growing up, we'll experiment with identities. Why? Because we want to feel safe and accepted, but the question we are asking is "who am I?" The bank of experiences we've had helps us paint a picture of how we believe life is, and our place in it. We aim to feel a sense of control and belonging, so we form identities that will distance us from pain and bring us closer to pleasure. For some that might mean becoming a perfectionist and studying obsessively hard. Others dress in a unique way or join a gang to fit in and feel a sense of belonging. Some of these experiments are healthy, others, not so healthy.

Think back over your life and see if you can recognise some of the different identities you adopted, and how those identities supported you. What clothes did you wear? What image did you want to portray? How important was your first car and how did it make you feel? Who did you like to associate with, where did you hang out, and what music did you listen to? What impression did you want to give the world at different times in your life? Our identity is related to our basic values and choices, but when we're growing up and even into adulthood, we often internalise the values of the dominant people and forces in our lives.

When I was eighteen, I had a boyfriend who was passionate about motorbikes. To be honest, I think he loved his bike more than he loved me. Even though I was under strict instructions from my parents not to ride pillion, I loved the thrill of being on the back of that bike. Of course, pushing the boundaries of parental discipline is a common way in which adolescents assert their identity.

At the tender age of eighteen, my boyfriend wasn't licensed to carry a passenger, so our travels were limited to dirt tracks and country lanes. One night we were riding home on a towpath alongside a river. Towpaths were used in times past for horses to haul boats or barges along the river but are now used as popular scenic walking paths. It was late and almost dark, and although the path was a narrow walking track that in the winter would be muddy and wet, it was easy riding in the dry summer months. I was enjoying being out in the open, feeling alive and carefree with the wind on my face, when suddenly I was shaken out of my relaxed state. As we hit a big dip there was a hard jolt through the bike and in an instant, we lurched up off the path and flew out over the river. It was a surreal moment as we were catapulted sideways, still perfectly seated on the bike but now gliding through the air!

This happened in the early 1980s, and as well as searching for my identity I was also extremely attached to a newly acquired pair of suede leather boots. They were knee-high with a heel, and by far the most prized footwear I had ever owned. These boots and the way I dressed at the time were an enormous part of the identity I wanted to portray as a teenager.

As we flew through the air destined for the cold water, time seemed to stand still and my thoughts in those seconds were very slow, very clear, and very much about my new suede boots! When I look back on this experience it seems incredible to me that in such a dangerous situation the only thing on my mind was the fact that my boots were about to be plunged into the dirty river. Not my life, nor that of my boyfriend, or even his expensive bike. No, my boots were my number one priority. Why? Probably because I felt like a million dollars in those boots and did not want that feeling to end.

I remember surfacing first and having a moment of panic because my boyfriend was nowhere to be seen. Then up he came, still with a hold on his bike. As I trod water and ripped off my treasured boots, throwing them up onto the towpath, he was desperately holding onto a major part of his identity, his motorbike. We walked home with our dented egos to persuade his sister and her boyfriend to bring their car and pull the bike from the river. I think that was probably the beginning of the end of that relationship because over the next few months fixing the bike became his number one priority.

As well as the different identities you've had, you've also had experiences that have left you feeling sad, inadequate, judged, angry, doubtful, helpless, vulnerable, embarrassed, or guilty, amongst other things. Maybe you've had a terribly traumatic experience or been on the receiving end of a throw-away line from a friend that cut you down and made you feel ostracised. This direct sensory information is learned and stored in a part of the brain called the amygdala. This happens without any conscious involvement from you, it's simply what happens; the amygdala's job is to take in this information and store it. The problem is that this stored information can control any future emotional responses. This connectivity is hard wired so when similar things look like they may happen, or a memory of those negative experiences is triggered, your body responds. Stress hormones are released, and you feel anxious because the unconscious mind is reminding you of things associated with this new event that's taking you out of your comfort zone.

This is what I call rummaging through your backpack. It's a completely unconscious process, in other words, we are not aware we're doing it. We are programmed to either move towards pleasure or away from pain, and this information is going to tell us which way to go. Remember 80% of our thoughts have a negative quality to them, so as we rummage through our backpack it's likely we'll find something that reminds us to be cautionary. When faced with a challenge that requires us to feel confident and capable our stored memory quickly reminds us of past confusion and humiliation, and says, "Watch out, that didn't turn out well last time, best not go there again."

You see, our radar is continually scanning to see how safe we are in any new situation. If you don't believe me, think about all the things in your life you've said you'll do but haven't done. Learn a language, travel the world, change career, set up a business, get fit, eat more healthily, move to another country, improve or change your relationship. Why do we procrastinate about these things when they are seemingly so important to us? It's because we stand on the road to our fullest potential and opportunity, unconsciously listening to the stories of doom and gloom from the past. "You'll never be able to do that!" "Don't bother; you don't have what it takes." "Forget it, it's too risky." The experiences from our past project a scene of future failure, and not surprisingly we become fearful and stuck. But read on and take heart, because your mind is not some deep, dark place waiting to trip you up, it's the source of your greatest power.

Chapter 6
You are in Control

Your mind is magnificent, its power and reach incredible; in fact, we are only just beginning to discover the brilliance of the human mind and how it can be used in positive ways. But for us to be in control of its brilliance we must learn to be aware of our unconscious thoughts by bringing them into consciousness. In other words, we must learn to focus our mind on the present moment rather than rummaging through that backpack of unconscious thoughts and beliefs. By doing this, we learn to distinguish between what is real and what is imagined. It sounds crazy, I know, but we spend most of our time lost in our imagination, and I don't mean imagining something lovely and relaxing, no, we're imagining an awful outcome to our problems, which causes worry, upset, and fear.

Think about it for a moment. What's your worst fear? Heights, deep water, being humiliated, confined spaces, appearing incompetent, going to the dentist, talking about your emotions, flying, spiders, snakes, hospitals, appearing foolish, public speaking? We've all had those moments in life when something stimulates an irrational fear, and we play it out for a few seconds until we feel the body reacting. We don't learn how to be afraid, but the amygdala, in the brain, learns what stimuli it should respond to. If I imagine a spider crawling up my arm, I feel my learned response kick in, my heart rate goes up and my body cringes. Especially if I imagine a large, hairy, Australian spider!

When we first came to live in Australia, I was told a lot of hair-raising stories about how large spiders have a habit of falling out from behind the sun visor in your car. Suffice it to say, I would check high and low for spiders before I got in my car. But my anxiety was caused by my imagination. I've never found a spider behind my sun visor, or anywhere else in my car for that matter, but I've had many cringe-worthy moments sitting at traffic lights wondering what's lurking under the dashboard. Now, we do have some dangerous spiders in Australia, but what I've learned to do with this, and other far more important challenges in my life, is to engage my conscious mind and bring my attention fully into the present moment.

When we focus on the reality of the present moment, rather than letting our imagination take over, we are back in control. It's our wandering mind that causes our anxiety. The mind tends to roam and make up stories that have us projecting into the future or ruminating about the past. But when we practice spending time with our mind calmly focused on the present moment, scientists are seeing an increase in a part of the brain called the hippocampus, which is responsible for conscious memory and perspective, and a decrease in the size of the amygdala. Remember, the amygdala is the emotional processing hub, and in very general terms learns how to respond to different stimuli based on its reference to embedded memory. It then makes decisions about emotional reactions based on this memory. This means that with practice we can grow the part of the brain that helps us gain perspective and shrink the part that's generating habitual and often unhelpful emotions.

If I were to ask you where your thoughts are in your body, you might say they're in your brain and you would be right to the extent that the brain picks up data and information, so that's where the stimulation begins. Imagine for a moment that you've come across a car accident. You survey the scene, and your brain processes the information, but that information stimulates a series of reactions that go way further than the brain. As you notice the severity of people's injuries and realise you are the only person around who can help, you begin to panic. Adrenaline starts to fill your body you begin to sweat and your breath becomes rapid. All this happens because you've started a conversation in your head that goes something like this: "Oh shit, I can't remember if I should move people, what am I meant to do first? All those first-aid courses I've done, come on think!" You start to question your capabilities because you just rummaged through your backpack of memories and beliefs and the message coming to you loud and clear is that you are NOT equipped to deal with this situation. In a split second your mind projects into the future and you see a scene in which you have failed in your responsibility to care for these people. These unconscious thoughts make you shake, your heart beats even faster and you can't think straight or compose yourself. Why? Because your mind is in your whole body, in every cell.

We have these unconscious conversations with ourselves all day long. Chatting about the dilemmas of life, other people, and ourselves. Check it out right now, it's the one you're having in your head as you process this information. It's the reason you occasionally need to go back a re-read a paragraph because your mind was elsewhere while you were trying to read. The problem is that these conversations and the associated stimulation in the body is what takes us out of the present and renders us distracted and confused. The most important thing to realise is that all these unconscious conversations are based either on the past or the future. We project and often worry about the future or ruminate and can regret the past. Little of our time is spent consciously in the present moment.

So, it would appear, if we could control the mind, life would be a whole lot easier. Well, basically, yes. We are conditioned from a young age to believe that our power, happiness, and success in life come from gaining control over our external environment. Often that's not possible, but what we do have real control over is our internal environment. The trick is to make your mind your best friend rather than your worst enemy.

Through my training and work as a meditation teacher and my own meditation practice, I've seen and experienced first-hand the myriad of ways in which gaining control of your mind can help you very gently and willingly move towards more of your potential. From relieving pain, dealing with health issues, healing relationships, stepping out of your comfort zone, or letting go of self-doubt, guilt, anger, or anxiety. Meditation enables us to identify when we are rummaging through that backpack of past experiences and buying into negativity, as we are prone to do.

Meditation is the pathway to remembering your true essence, that bulb of pure potential, still carrying your backpack of experiences, which make up the rich tapestry of your life, but undaunted by their stories. This enables you to stand in the eye of any storm, observing your mind play its 3D, multi-coloured movie show of past failings and future disasters, and let it all move through you as you respond with control.

Imagine if you came across the same car accident that I mentioned earlier, but this time you have the understanding and skills to know that to be at your best you must take immediate action to control your debilitating inner conversations, doubts and fears. Now you can think clearly, your emotions are under control and your physical reserves are strong. The resources you need to save lives are readily available because you dealt with your inner world rather than trying to frantically help people whilst chaos reigned in your mind and body.

Meditation shows you the value of putting your oxygen mask on first! It teaches you that most of what is in your backpack won't help you unless you look upon those life events with compassion and understanding and use them to grow. It shows you that what you vividly imagine about your disastrous future most likely isn't going to happen. It's all in your mind. And meditation teaches us that wherever we stand on our road to potential is a unique and new moment, deserving of our conscious, controlled, and composed attention.

I have a quote on my office wall by an unknown author that says "Peace. It does not mean to be in a place where there is no noise, trouble, or hard work. It means to be in the midst of those things and still be calm in your heart." It's worth a try, don't you think?

For much of my life, I've been curious about the mind and the eastern philosophies advocating meditation to find peace and happiness. I've been fortunate to have some wise and knowledgeable teachers in my life, and my exposure to yoga has helped me on this journey. I've grown to understand the power of the mind as a force that has a huge impact on health and well-being, and the value of being in control of it. Meditation and other practices that enable me to manage my mind proactively have become an integral part of my life. I'm delighted to see that some schools are integrating meditation into their curriculums. I believe it's a life skill that has the power to positively impact the world.

Since I've experienced the benefits of meditation and the innate ability I have to control my mind, it astonishes me that we readily use our minds to scare ourselves to death, but we rarely use them to help us feel safe, happy, and optimistic. This is a key point I teach in my courses, and time and again women tell me how liberated they feel through the simple understanding that most of their worries and anxieties are caused by their thoughts about a situation, not by the situation itself.

The thing is, it only takes a short time each day to train your mind to be your best friend rather than your worst enemy. It takes a few minutes each morning to lay down healthy thought processes, and the foundations of a clear, calm sense of well-being that will help carry you successfully through your day. Yet most people would rather start their day with ten minutes of depressing news, another stimulating coffee, or a trawl through pointless social media. Later in the book, I'll show you a simple morning ritual that will help you begin each day in a way that supports your well-being.

The good news is you are in control. I know it doesn't feel that way at times! But I'm going to show you some practices that will help to ensure that a sense of control becomes second nature to you. The bad news is that this control requires that you take full responsibility for the way you think, feel, and act. It requires that you demonstrate self-compassion and self-awareness, which I believe are the two most important steppingstones to potential.

The concept of self-awareness was defined by Shelley Duval and Robert Wicklund, authors of the book, *A Theory of Objective Self-awareness*. They noted, "... when we focus our attention on ourselves, we evaluate and compare our current behaviour to our internal standards and values. We become self-conscious as objective evaluators of ourselves." The more self-aware we become, the greater our capacity to respond to challenges in life rather than react to them. We learn to direct our attention away from the supposed external cause of our problems and instead consciously and objectively assess what we are thinking and feeling and what action we could take.

One of our innate, but often forgotten qualities emerge when we learn to approach life's challenges from the perspective of internal enquiry rather than external resistance. We realise that we have a reservoir of self-compassion and the ability to respond lovingly and kindly to ourselves and others, instead of being chained to our habitual unhelpful reactions. Self-compassion is the ability to act toward yourself with loving-kindness when faced with such things as conflict, doubt, and fear. It's about honing the ability to treat yourself with the same kind, considerate care that you would offer your best friend.

Dr. Kirsten Neff, the author of the book *Self Compassion,* describes it as having three elements: self-kindness vs self-judgment, common humanity vs isolation, and mindfulness vs over-identification. This means being kind, gentle, and understanding toward ourselves when we fail, rather than ignoring our pain or punishing ourselves with self-criticism. Understanding that all humans suffer and realising that suffering and feeling inadequate is part of the shared human experience. And being willing to observe our negative thoughts and not be hooked by our habitual, unconscious, negative reactivity. As you'll discover, this kinder approach to understanding our fears and failures holds enormous power and potential.

Remember I told you that my teacher berated me in front of my friends? She and I at that moment were not demonstrating self-awareness or self-compassion. Perhaps she felt overwhelmed by her responsibility to ensure her students pass their exams, or maybe she was tired and reacted at that moment. I didn't have the self-awareness or self-compassion skills that I do now and chose to process that interaction negatively. Because I didn't know any better, that situation and others have manifested in my life as doubt about my academic ability. I'm not condoning thoughtless behaviour, but as we do the necessary work of managing the biggest obstacle to our potential - our mind - we begin to understand that everyone is trying their best. We realise that inner criticism will never help us to succeed in the long term and that identifying with our negative thoughts will always result in reactivity. And we realise that we are all the same at our core and share the same human experience. We were all born as pure potential and ventured out on our life journey getting knocked and battered along the way. Everyone you meet is continually adjusting their course, narrowing their path when they feel vulnerable, or striding confidently down it when they are coping well and feel a sense of control. At our core we are love, but we allow many of the experiences we have in life to draw us away from love and keep us locked in fear.

The question is, how do we become adept at ensuring our mind is our best friend? How do we engage with the rich tapestry of thoughts, memories, and emotions that we experience in our lives in a way that is informative and supportive; instead of listening to the voice of our inner critic reminding us of our inadequacies and restrictions? How do we learn to manage this magnificent machine called the mind and live from love rather than fear?

As human beings, we are comprised of four main aspects: intellectual, emotional, physical, and spiritual. Having greater awareness of the rich information your mind and body provide will enable you to maintain balance and well-being across these human qualities. In my experience women often allow their well-being to get pushed to the bottom of their long list of priorities and find themselves surviving rather than thriving. But by taking simple steps to care for your well-being you'll be able to manage your inner world and navigate the inevitable challenges of your life with more clarity, control, and confidence. Fostering awareness and stability in these four aspects will ensure that your journey down the road of life will be one of growth and enjoyment, rather than resistance and pain. You'll have more control over the way you think, feel, and act and be inspired and optimistic at the prospect of reaching more of your potential.

Chapter 7
Back Flips

Let's begin by discerning exactly what potential is? The dictionary definition of the word potential is, "Having or showing the capacity to develop into something in the future."

Potential is not a destination to be reached, it's a moment-by-moment, hour-by-hour, day-by-day, month-by-month, year-by-year unfolding of your capacity to develop into "something." Whatever you decide you want to develop into. Isn't that exciting? There may be no medals, praise, or fame as you develop, but there will be growth in your abilities, greater confidence, and a sense of purpose and self-worth. I remember my father trying to tell me this when I was a teenager; he told me there are two kinds of people in the world, those who try and those who don't. What he wanted me to understand was that a good school grade wasn't the only thing to aim for, it was in my endeavour and attitude that I'd also get my reward. If I'd understood this message more clearly and had the skills to foster a sense of greater self-worth and confidence, the journey of attempting to reach more of my potential would have been inspiring and satisfying, even when I didn't get an A+. For generations, we've been trying to foster potential and success in children within a school system that requires them to pitch themselves against each other and be judged better or worse than the next person. And that's likely how you've been conditioned, as well.

When I would read my school reports at the back of the bus, not only was I disillusioned by my inability to reach this elusive state of potential, I was also comparing my grades and the remarks in my report with my friends. When we compare ourselves to others and measure our success against other people, all the while looking outside ourselves for recognition and approval, our ability to access our potential is greatly diminished. The road we travel will always be much harder when we fail to understand that a gratifying journey towards our goals and dreams requires that we take full responsibility for how we manage our thoughts, feelings, and emotions.

Remember that wide-open road of life we talked about, the one that holds your potential and has no end. That's because there is no end to your capacity to develop into something in the future.

You may want to be a better mother, a more caring daughter, a successful business owner, a compassionate friend, a world-renowned scientist, a kinder boss, a public speaker, a world leader, a better cook, a healthier version of you, or someone who has more self-compassion. There are many areas of our lives where we can strive for and sometimes even feel we are reaching our potential. But how do we ever know? I think it's a very personal thing.

At the age of 53, I took up rowing for the first time. Now, I'm not sure if you're familiar with the sport of rowing but the boats are narrow, light, and tip over very easily! But I'm pretty game when it comes to sporting activities. More kudos to Mr. Skelton who was not only my history teacher but my sports teacher as well. When I was thirteen one of the most thrilling things in my life was gymnastics and one of the most exhilarating moments in my gym class was when I did my first backflip. It was not life-changing in the grand scheme of things but a memorable moment in my life. Week after week, with the patience of a saint, Mr. Skelton knelt on the gym mat next to me encouraging me to throw myself backward. I'd hold my arms out then swing them down by my side and bend my knees, ready to throw them back up again to get the momentum to propel myself up off my feet. Then I'd stop, just as I was about to take off, too scared that I'd fall on my head. Mr. Skelton encouraged me as I faltered over and again or fell in a crumpled heap on the mat. Then finally, I did it. Landing that backflip was a moment in time when for a split second I felt I'd reached my potential. As I felt my hands touch the ground, I knew I'd nailed it. My legs came effortlessly over the top and I sprung upright balanced and composed, with both feet firmly planted next to each other on the blue plastic mat. I was euphoric.

You know that feeling, even if you haven't done a backflip, you've achieved something in your life that for a moment made you want to squeal with delight. It's a great feeling and one that inspires us to keep going. Soon my backflips felt like second nature and then the realisation set in that I could try and do two backflips in a row. Onward! You see, we just can't help ourselves, we have an innate desire to keep moving forward. At thirteen, one backflip wasn't enough for me. I wanted to discover more of my ability.

In 1976 I spent a lot of my time at a local gymnastics club. The Romanian gymnast Nadia Comaneci was my hero, and that same year she landed a perfect score of ten for her performance on the uneven bars at the Montreal Olympics. Now, if we're measuring potential, I'd say she'd reached hers at that point. But did she stop there? No, she went on to record a perfect 10 six more times and became the youngest all-around Olympic gold medallist ever. Continually striving for more of her potential.

Rowing is one sport for sure where I will be striving to reach more of my potential until I'm too old and decrepit to get in a boat! Rowing has taught me the true meaning of potential. I'm a late starter and am often racing against women who are far more experienced than I am. I'm pleased with myself when I can sit on the start line without hyperventilating, keep my technique, stay in my lane, and make it to the finish line. But I love it because it's a great lesson in inner composure and a wonderful metaphor for life. You see, the more distracted I become by the very fit and composed-looking competitors alongside me and the more I listen to the voices in my head telling me I've got no chance, the more anxious I get. Then I become tense, and the tenser I get the worse my rowing technique gets, and the slower my boat goes. But, when I concentrate on quietening my inner critic, the intellectual aspect that chats away, calming my nerves and soothing the emotional aspect that gets churned up, my physical body relaxes. Then I'm able to use my energy to row, rather than it all being expended by my elevated heart rate and my tense body.

Just as in everyday life, when we attend to our thoughts and emotions and find inner composure, confidence follows and life flows with far more ease. Even though my thoughts tell me I probably won't win the race, whenever I sit on the start line, I get a stark life lesson that inner composure will win every time over fighting an outer battle with reality. And I experience another step on the never-ending path of potential.

You see, the journey never ends. Look at your own life right now. Some things are important to you that you want to improve, or you may feel frustrated or dissatisfied with other areas of your life, be it a relationship, a job, a business, a friendship, a hobby, your health, or your finances. These feelings you have about wanting to move or change or improve, have you reaching for more of your potential. It's a natural and never-ending journey because there's no end game. Ability is a never-ending, constantly evolving process of growing into something in the future, and an innate feature of being human. External cheer-leading and motivation is helpful but can only get you so far. To reach greater heights and more importantly enjoy the journey, inner blocks must be cleared so you can become self-reliant and tap into your inner power of potential, independent of external circumstances. When you learn to trust the more passive approach of going within and checking out your mind and body, just like I've done on the start line of a rowing race, you'll find inner calm, encouragement, and inspiration. This inner approach will drown out the voice of dejection and indifference and be more helpful than external cheerleading ever will.

Some of us have had a relatively easy run into adulthood, while others have been battered by life with greater obstacles to overcome. Your journey thus far has been unique and personal, and what you want to develop into at this stage in your life is also deeply personal and unique to you. We're all on our own journey, desiring different experiences. As you begin to explore where you want to reach for more of your potential, you may already be noticing how easily your mind compares you to others. We have a habit of looking at what others have achieved and instead of gaining inspiration from them, we'll often judge ourselves negatively. As Theodore Roosevelt said, unfavourable comparison to others can be the thief of joy, and I believe a complete de-motivator when trying to reach more of your potential and be successful in life. Be mindful of that sneaky, disdainful voice that starts comparing you to someone else and tells you your goals aren't lofty enough, or the other voice that tells you not to bother because you don't have the talent and will never succeed. Or the one that tells you it's all too hard and keeps you locked in procrastination.

You may not want to climb Everest, but you may want to develop into a person who is eager to get out of bed in the morning and feel excited about life. You don't have to be parent of the year, but you may want to develop into someone who no longer gets angry with your children. You may not want to build a multinational corporation, but perhaps you have a desire to build a business where people love to work and you're improving the world. Maybe you want to get fit, become a better artist, learn to swim, be more attentive to your children or loving to your partner, lose 10 kilos, or stop feeling guilty, grumpy, or resentful. The life journey you are on holds multiple possibilities for more happiness and success. The key is to ensure you embark on that journey with some resources in place that will enable the journey to unfold with ease and inspiration, rather than struggle and stress.

Unless we do the inner work required to ensure we are feeling a strong sense of self-worth and inner resilience, we will always be at the mercy of past conditioning that can keep us locked in self-doubt, fear, and unfavourable comparison to others.

PART II

Chapter 8
The Four Aspects

The four aspects of being human are intellectual, physical, emotional, and spiritual. (In this context, spiritual does not mean religious, rather it is the imaginative, creative, loving, connecting, inspirational part of us.) Society conditions us to believe that driving ourselves and pushing through at all costs is the key to fulfilling more of our potential. Of course, the action is required, but the first key to fulfilling more potential lies in doing the inner work necessary to maintain health in each of these human aspects. Unless we do, our attempts can take a huge toll on our happiness and our health. We all have a preference as to which of these aspects we feel most comfortable in, and this is where we spend most of our time.

Within each of these aspects, we can experience either health or dis-ease. All aspects are intricately interwoven and no one aspect stands alone, as each affects the other. We can either ignore our inner world, enduring our habitual, unhelpful behaviour that will often lead to a downward spiral of despair; or we can proactively enhance our understanding and healing of these aspects to gain clarity, composure, energy, and purpose, that will propel us on an upward spiral of potential.

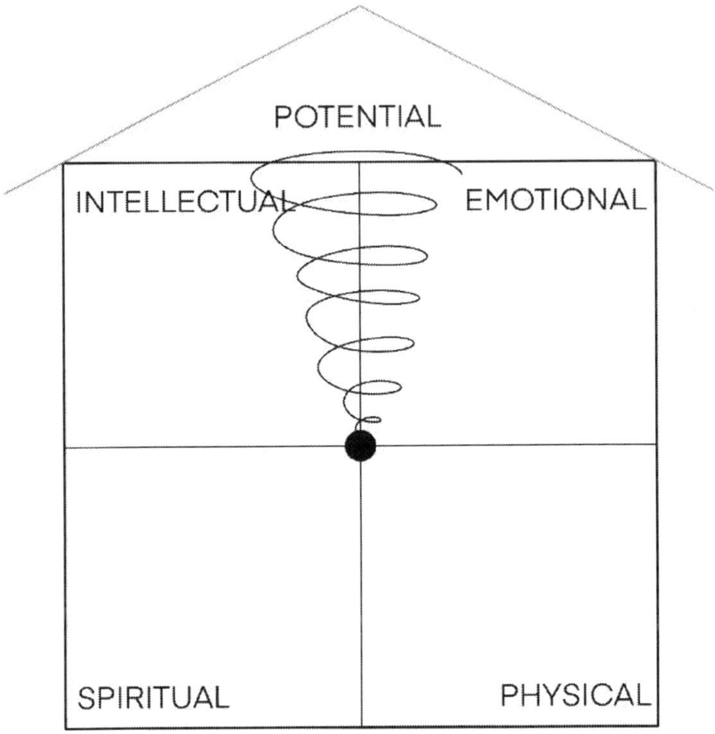

Figure 1: The Upward Spiral of Potential – *showing the four aspects of well-being that need to be addressed to stay on an upward spiral of potential.*

We're going to get back to this model later. For now, just be aware that you are comprised of intellect, emotion, physicality, and spirit. First, let's identify some areas in your life where you're ready for more potential. Meaning, you're ready to unlock your capacity to develop into something more in the future. Often when we think about potential we think of big tangible goals, which is why I want to reiterate that this book is for all women, whatever it is in your life that you'd like to develop is important and will be unique to you.

In the context of these four aspects of being human, this first exercise will enable you to do a "health check" on how you currently perceive your level of potential, success, and happiness in different areas of your life. Most women don't take the time to actively consider the condition of their health, happiness, relationships, work, or life purpose. Women spend a lot of time nurturing and caring for others, which can mean their needs don't get addressed until something goes wrong. I've seen this pattern over and again in myself, my family, my friends, and the people I work with, waiting until we are faced with real discomfort, turmoil, or disease before we are forced to stop and take stock of our inner world. Perhaps you've already been thrown the curveball and are facing some genuine challenges, or maybe you know deep inside that you've become complacent and there's room for improvement in certain areas of your life. If so, this process will help you tease them out. Or perhaps life is good, and you want to proactively ensure it stays that way. Whatever your current situation, it's always revealing and therapeutic to do some honest soul searching and write down your insights.

You can approach this exercise from a negative or a positive angle. If it makes it easier, think about what you're dissatisfied with. What are you putting up with, feeling unhappy, worried, or guilty about? What are you frustrated, or fed up with? Or, come at it from the positive angle, how would you like to feel, what qualities do you want to bring to your health, your relationships, and work? Where would you like to be in one, five, or ten years from now? What skills do you want to hone, abilities would you like to improve, or friendships do you want to deepen?

Under each of the headings below identify some areas where you know you have latent qualities or abilities that could be developed and lead to greater success and happiness in your life. There are no rules about how you write this out. If you're a list person, make a list; if you'd prefer to use free-flow writing, that's fine too. The idea is to address all areas of your life and get all your thoughts onto the page. To make this worthwhile, set aside some time when you won't be disturbed. Get a pen and notebook ready, then sit quietly with your eyes closed and take some nice deep breaths. Spend a few minutes focusing on your breath, sigh occasionally, let go of tension, relax your body, and bring yourself to a state of calm focus before you begin to write.

If doing this exercise leads to other thoughts, feelings, and ideas that you feel compelled to write about, go ahead and do that too. Take as much time as you need. This exercise can be very revealing and inspirational so ensure you have the time to write more if you want to.

Exercise 2 - The 4 Aspects Health Check

1) **In the area of Health and Well-Being, where are you feeling enthused to reach more of your potential?**

For example –

Would you like to feel more competent intellectually and improve your critical thinking or memory? Would you like to be a calmer, more composed person, or feel more capable, optimistic, and happy? Would you like to be fitter, have more energy or address a health issue? Or would you like to experience a deeper connection to yourself and others or have more purpose and meaning in your life? What do you want to stop doing and what would you like to start doing around health and well-being?

Your answer might say -

I want to feel more confident and not doubt my intellectual ability. I want to be a more optimistic person with more energy and enthusiasm for life. I want to find more purpose and meaning in my life.

2) **In the area of Relationships, where do you feel inspired to improve?**

For example -

Would you like to improve the quality of your relationship with yourself, your spouse, or your partner? Perhaps you feel concerned about your relationship with your children, parents, siblings, friends, or colleagues and want to change this.

Your answer might say -

I would like to take time to nurture and look after myself without feeling guilty. I want to have a closer, more intimate relationship with my partner and have more fun with my children.

3) **Work / Business / Career / Study / Finances**

For example -

How do you feel about your level of satisfaction and success in your career or business? Are you seeking more education or advancement in your work? How do you feel about your income and savings? Are you happy with the level of stability in your life? What about your motivation, interest, and passion for your study or work?

Your answer might say -

I want to find a career that enables me to feel I'm doing some good in the world. I would like more financial stability in my life and time to study a language.

4) **Friends / Social Life / Community / Wider world**

For example -

How would you rate the quality of your friendships and social life? Do you have like-minded, interesting people in your circle of friends and colleagues? Do you feel supported and inspired by your friends and are you inspiring and supportive to your friends? Are you satisfied with your level of engagement in your community? Is there some way you'd like to contribute to the wider world?

Your answer might say -

I'd like to have a group of friends who challenge me and support my personal growth. I want to be more engaged with my wider community in a meaningful way by....

5) **Hobbies / Interests / Bucket List / Travel / Volunteer**

For example -

How satisfied are you with your level of engagement and enjoyment around your hobbies and interests? Are there new hobbies you'd like to start or something you want to learn? Have you ticked anything off your bucket list in the last two years? Are you putting off volunteering or travelling? What dreams and desires have you shelved?

Your answer might say -

I want to spend more time enjoying – *insert hobby* - without feeling guilty. I want to see more of the world and volunteer at my local soup kitchen.

Keep this exercise as a living document, revisit it often, and add to it any thoughts or feelings you have about the various aspects of your life. Take note of the insights and messages that come to you as you write. Later in the book, I'll show you how you can use meditation to help you foster a more positive and balanced mindset around some of these aspects of your life that you'd like to improve.

Journalling is a very revealing and cathartic process and can help the mind begin to make sense of things that can seem overwhelming or confusing. I encourage you to write your thoughts down daily. Sit down to your blank page with no expectation, simply fill the page with your thoughts. It doesn't matter if they don't make sense, once out on the written page, they have been bought into consciousness. This in itself is a powerful healing process. As you journal more and work your way through this book, it will hopefully become more obvious why you have areas of dissatisfaction in your life or are ignoring an inner calling. You're going to discover tools and techniques that will put you in a healthier frame of mind and enable you to enjoy your life more.

We move between the intellectual, emotional, physical, and spiritual parts of ourselves rapidly, moment by moment, and life circumstances require that we visit an aspect when we may not wish to. We also develop a preference for one or two aspects over others and can be reluctant to visit our less favoured ones.

There's an Indian proverb that says "Everyone is a house with four rooms, mental, emotional, physical and spiritual. Most of us tend to live in one room most of the time but unless we go into every room every day, even if only to keep it aired, we are not a complete person."

I'm going to show you how to go into all those rooms and air them out, so you can unlock your potential and find greater success and happiness in the areas of your life that are important to you. *Please note that I'll be referring to the mental room as the "intellectual aspect."*

Life is never going to stop challenging us in one way or another but when we're healthy intellectually, emotionally, physically, and spiritually, we become skilled at keeping our unhelpful thoughts and beliefs about our past, and our negative imaginings about our future, in check. We learn to live more mindfully and allow our emotions to move through us like a gentle wave rather than crash in like a storm. And we have a deeper connection to the important messages and signals our physical body produces that often go unheard.

When we are healthy in all aspects, we can unlock our enormous capacity to respond to life's ups and downs with grace and composure. We regain the trust in life that we felt in our childhood before we bought into our doubts and fears. We enjoy more ease, flow and faith in ourselves, others, and life, and can tap into energy and inspiration that enables us to connect to something greater than ourselves. Ironically, this whole process is a reflective inward journey of letting go that is at odds with our culture of action and doing. But getting a handle on our inner world enables us to gain real control, rather than habitually pushing and stressing our way through life, which only creates the illusion of control. Doing this inner passive work lays strong foundations from where we are far more likely to enjoy successful outer action in the world.

Let's look at each aspect in more detail and discover how to foster their healthy qualities so you can begin to enjoy some ease and flow in your life. This next step requires you to have an open mind. I'm inviting you to consider that taking care of yourself intellectually, emotionally, physically, and spiritually will put you firmly on the path to your potential, in a way that external push, drive, and motivation alone never can.

Chapter 9
The Intellectual Aspect

The intellectual aspect is the logical, analytical thinking part of you. When in full health it operates with clarity, focus, and attention. Our intellectual aspect is concerned with taking in data and conveying information in a logical, clear, concise manner. When this aspect is out of balance, we can feel distracted and confused, and I'm sure you've also experienced times in your life when the intellectual aspect of you has been firing on all cylinders. These are the times when the acuity of attention comes easily to you, information can be quickly and effortlessly absorbed, and the thinking analytical mind lights up like a Christmas tree! When we're out of balance in this aspect we can feel chaotic, unclear, and muddled.

So, why do we have chaotic thoughts and get distracted? Let's go back to the road you were visualising earlier. Imagine that along each side of your road there are many trees lined up, side by side and in the branches of those trees are thousands of birds. Now, I'm not talking about tweeting little brown birds, think loud, big, squawking birds. For those of you who've been to Australia, you'll know what I mean!

Cockatoos are a family of large very noisy parrots, of which there are fourteen species in Australia. The common ones are white with a large yellow crest, a grey beak, and dark round eyes. Equally at home in the city or the countryside, these raucous birds are curious and friendly, and you always know when they are in the neighbourhood because they make a hell of a racket!

My husband and I love to camp and when we do, we can guarantee there will be cockatoos around. As I lie in our tent ready to sleep, I can hear them in a nearby tree, chatting away as the last of the light fades. Just like some human conversations they start quietly, then more and more birds join in until it seems they are having a screaming match, before it quietens down again. This routine goes on repeatedly until finally they rest. But not for long. Before the sun comes up, they are at it again, immediately busy as they furiously squawk at each other. We have struck some camping spots off our list due to the incessant noise of the resident birds. When we're home it's not uncommon for a lone cockatoo to fly by our house squawking loudly, seemingly to herself.

This is not unlike what goes on in your head day after day. From the moment you wake up you have unchecked conversations squawking in your head. You'll notice it more at times when you're quiet; for example, I notice it when I go for a run or a walk. I'll be jogging along having a full conversation in my head, which is usually a rehearsal of something to come or a rework of a conversation I've already had. Believe it or not, another good time to catch these conversations is when you're cleaning your teeth or taking a shower. Give it a go next time you're in the bathroom.

Imagine if you could tell those birds to fly away and you could drop into a space where you're able to think clearly and feel a sense of calm, composed control, even during the most testing and upsetting times of your life. With a little practice, it's possible to quiet those conversations in your head and ride out the storms of life with a lot less angst. In the process ensuring your physical body isn't put under needless pressure.

Many of the thoughts and conversations that we have with ourselves are informed by the data we carry around in our backpacks full of memories, attitudes and behaviour patterns. The enormous part of the mind called the unconscious is where all these memories are stored. The unconscious mind holds our biography, beliefs, and habits. It's an information provider that most of the time is on autopilot. Studies show that between 95% - 97% of the mind is operating in this unconscious way, which means that very few of our thoughts have to do with what is going on in the present moment.

Even though I bought this to your attention earlier, I bet again, while reading this book, at some point you recognised you were thinking about something other than the information on the page. You either skipped over that section or went back and read it with more focus. I know I'm not doing a great sales job on my book by highlighting your lack of attention, but I'm willing to take that hit so you can see how unreliable your mind can be. This happens because while you've been trying to take in information about onions, backpacks, and imaginary roads, your birds have been chatting away about the state of your bank balance, what you forgot to do today, what you need to remember for tomorrow, how annoyed you are at your work colleague or the kids, and so the chat goes on. Go ahead and check out the conversations in your head right now, see what you're chatting to yourself about. And if you're thinking, "I don't have conversations in my head," that's the conversation I'm talking about!

The problem is that these conversations are usually unconscious, in other words, we don't consciously hear them. Unconsciously we take in what they have to say and let their content dictate our thoughts, feelings, emotions, and behaviours. Unless, through practices such as meditation, we train ourselves to become more aware or conscious of these conversations and the impact they can have on us.

My younger son has always been an adventurer and due to modern technology, I can see many of these adventures online. When he was nineteen and travelling around Vietnam, I saw a picture of him on Facebook, he was on a motorbike wearing shorts, flip flops, and a helmet that looked about as useful as a bucket. As a mother my mind went into overdrive. I'm not exactly sure what I was thinking, because when this happens the thoughts come thick and fast, but what I immediately felt was a knot in my stomach and a sense of fear wash over me. That night I realised that the story I'd been telling myself had him in a hospital with my husband and I flying to Vietnam to bring him home battered and broken. The absurdity of this situation is, that while I'd been worrying, he had arrived at his destination safely and was enjoying his holiday, not before ditching the bike helmet. Thank goodness I didn't know that! Of course, my motherly protection kicked in as any parents would when you see your child in potential danger. But added to that, my mind had made up a catastrophic story that caused me a lot of unnecessary angst. Meanwhile, my son was having the time of his life.

Thoughts can instigate a conversation in our head at any time about anything and everything. From how our kids should be behaving, how we compare to our work colleagues, whether we can afford the mortgage, whether we should be promoted, to what's wrong with our relationship, other people, or our life, on and on it goes, day in and day out. Remember we have thousands of thoughts every day, many of them repetitive and many that have a negative quality to them. It's these thoughts that prompt conversations in our heads, and as we're discovering, most of these thoughts are based in the past or the future. So, apart from the fact that we are missing most of the treasured moments of our lives while we waste our time ruminating or rehearsing, it's also exhausting intellectually, emotionally, physically, and spiritually.

What we're going to learn to do is to become more conscious of these thoughts and conversations. Why? So we can gain some control over our thought processes. When we are more conscious of our thoughts it changes everything because we gain insight and awareness into the inner workings of our mind. It's the first step to making your mind your best friend instead of your worst enemy.

As I imagined my youngest son in a mangled bike accident in a third-world country my intellectual aspect was in an unhealthy state. My thoughts were muddled, and I was not thinking logically or questioning with reason and rationale. The moment the mind starts playing its multi-coloured movie of doom and gloom is a vital point of discernment. Whether worrying about our children, fretting about our finances, angry with our partner, or upset about a comment made by a colleague; unless we can recognise that the story our mind is making up has become more dominant than the truth, we've lost control. This feeling of losing control intensifies our negative experience even more, and we begin a spiral down to despair. I believe this critical point of awareness is life-changing. It denotes the difference between tapping into our true nature of compassion and love, from where we can resourcefully respond to a situation, or getting trapped by fear and letting our habitual negative reactions play out.

The emotional and physical aspects come out in response to our thoughts. When the intellectual aspect is immersed in negative thoughts, emotions are triggered, and the physical body responds to these emotions. You see, your poor body doesn't know whether what you're thinking is real or not. It simply responds to the emotions stimulated by the stories your mind makes up. If those stories are of doom and gloom, then the physical body will react with symptoms of stress such as a raised heart rate, nervous stomach aches, and muscle tension. You know the story.

Chapter 10
The Emotional Aspect

All negative emotions are based on fear. The fear that we'll make a fool of ourselves, fear we'll look incapable, fear of being wrong, fear we won't be accepted or liked, fear we're not loved or that we're not in control, even fear that we'll succeed. Fear was what I was feeling as I looked at that image of my son on his motorbike in his shorts and flip-flops. But do you see how I was exacerbating the problem? I was adding my embellishments, hairpin bends on mountain roads, reckless drivers, horrific injuries, and third-world hospitals. Whether the trigger had come from a photo, someone telling me about the motorbike trip, or it just crossed my mind; once that seed had been planted I was perfectly capable of making up a multicoloured, three-D movie of doom and gloom with this wonderful thing we have called the mind. The mind is an amazing thing, the trick is to learn how to use it to gain control rather than allow it to be in control.

Let's stop for a moment and ponder the importance of this. There are three things that we human beings do have complete control over if we choose. Those three things are our thoughts, our feelings/emotions, and our actions. Some of you may be questioning whether you have control over your emotions, or whether they come and go as they please, without any bidding from you.

If this is a new concept for you, I urge you to keep an open mind. If you get nothing from this book other than the understanding that you are in control of your emotions and can choose how you feel at any given moment, I'll be happy, because that knowledge alone will positively change your life.

Of course, I'm not suggesting that you never feel undesirable emotions. There are times in our lives when we grieve and there are times when trauma or change can disturb the balance of our lives so much that we are consumed with sadness or despair. Allowing these emotions to move through us is an important part of healing. But it's also important to discern when we have become stuck and embedded a negative emotion so deeply in our mind-body system that it informs our way of being and clouds our life experience.

As we grow up, the information in our unconscious mind begins to run the show, and as we've discussed we tend to draw upon the negative memories held there. These memories keep us well and truly in our place as far as our level of confidence, self-worth, self-esteem, and beliefs about our capabilities are concerned. Not to mention our limited capacity for self -compassion. When we experience negative emotions, such as when we feel upset, afraid, inadequate, or incapable, it's not only because a challenging event has occurred, but because this event sparks negative memories of similar past experiences held in our unconscious mind.

When I was in primary school, we were separated into groups according to our ability in mathematics. I can remember sitting at a round table in the corner of the room with our headmaster and a small group of children. It was a cosy corner of the library, the sun was streaming in through the window, and I can vividly remember feeling quite excited about this new situation I found myself in. I particularly liked the round table and the fact that we were in a more intimate group and I liked our headmaster, so I felt very special. Until I realised that I was special in a way that you don't want to be! After a few of these maths sessions, it became clear to me that we hadn't been singled out because we were special, we'd been singled out because we needed extra help, and were holding back the rest of the class. I understood clearly that we were different, and in my young mind, I decided there was something wrong with me. I filed this thought and the corresponding emotions of embarrassment and inadequacy away in my unconscious mind, often allowing it to come out and plague me well into my adult life. I can laugh about this now, and I'm delighted to think that in my young, optimistic mind I initially believed that our little maths group was truly special. I'm sure much of that was because our headmaster at the time did make us feel special.

The term "special needs" wasn't a part of the educational vocabulary in the sixties; it's now thankfully a well-established practice in primary schools in first-world countries to have special needs teachers or aides, and it would be wonderful if all children who need it had this assistance. However, labelling people and especially children at such a young and impressionable age can be very detrimental to the way they see themselves and their capabilities. At some stage, a special-needs child will realise that this type of special isn't desirable, and they'll form an opinion about themselves based on that information. That opinion will be filed away in the unconscious mind, what we're referring to as our backpack of life stories. That story has the power to colour a person's outlook and belief in themselves, often for the rest of their lives, just as my first experience of being segregated into a 'special' maths learning group has coloured my life. Unless we do the inner work necessary and uncover the truth!

As I've said, the mind is an amazing thing. Imagine how much easier and freer the path to your potential would be if only you would use your mind in a more positive and powerful way. The mind is not a dark, sinister place waiting to trip you up, but you do need to proactively train it to be your friend and harness its power. Imagine if you could ride out the challenges of your life feeling calm and composed. Imagine how different your life would be if the beliefs you held about yourself and the emotions you experienced were of your own choice, inspiring, comforting, and uplifting, rather than the sorry tales dredged up from your unconscious mind. Well, they can be, with a little practice. When you're not paying attention, unhelpful thoughts and emotions can settle into your system like a well-worn jacket. They become part of you, and you become so used to this way of being that those childhood experiences of unbridled love of life and trust become a dim and distant memory.

Chapter 11
The Physical Aspect

Any emotion we experience impacts the physical body and positive thoughts and emotions can have a regenerative effect. But the emotions that arise from our negative thoughts such as self-doubt, anger, frustration, worry, resentment, shame, or guilt can have a degenerative effect on the physical body. The physical body doesn't know whether what you are experiencing is real or not, it simply responds to incoming stimulus. Remember those birds chattering away all day in the trees? The stories they tell you are clear and vivid. They are stories about you, someone, or something else, they are either positive or negative and are mostly based on the past or the future. Check it out for yourself now, what's going on in your life that you're mulling over? As you think about it, you'll be replaying what's already passed or imagining what's to come, or both. Now, don't get me wrong, there is a time and a place for thinking things through, understanding a situation to the best of your ability, discerning how you feel about it, and deciding what action you want to take. The problem is, we don't compartmentalise the unhelpful conversations and we're not prone to proactively managing the emotions they evoke. They're like a broken record that plays away in the background. And we wonder why we feel emotionally troubled and physically challenged.

When you're feeling disturbed, upset, or downright angry about an incident that's occurred in your life, the emotions you feel about that event will trigger certain responses in the body via what is known as the involuntary or autonomic nervous system. There are two systems within the autonomic nervous system, the sympathetic and the parasympathetic system. The sympathetic nervous system will direct your body's rapid, involuntary response to any threatening or stressful situations. You'll be able to recall a time when your sympathetic nervous system kicked in, maybe when you narrowly missed hitting another car, or without realising you stepped out in front of oncoming traffic. Perhaps you can recall a time when you had an impending deadline and felt unprepared and overwhelmed. If you're like me and afraid of heights, you'll feel this system kick in any time you're on the edge of a cliff or a tall building. You may have heard the term fight-or-flight, which is how this system is described. Without conscious direction and very quickly our fight-or-flight system kicks in when we feel we're in danger. It's a system that's important for our very survival.

Our mind-body system is an amazing communication network of brain structures, receptors, nerves, and hormones that process signals from the body and tune the activity of the autonomic nervous system in response. When we feel we're in danger, this communication network instructs a flood of hormones, such as adrenaline and cortisol, to be released to boost alertness. The heart rate goes up, sending extra blood to the muscles, the breath quickens, sending fresh oxygen to the brain and a cocktail of glucose is released into the bloodstream for a quick energy boost. All of this happens very rapidly so we can react quickly to the dangerous situation we're in. In these situations, the body is working hard and fast and we might feel our heart beating out of our chest or experience shortness of breath or sweating.

The other component of the autonomic nervous system is called the parasympathetic nervous system and works to calm the body down. The job of this system is to counter the fight-or-flight response. It is also known as the "rest-and-digest" system because this is what it encourages the body to do. Blood pressure, breathing, and hormone flow all have a chance to come back to equilibrium as this system does its work.

These two systems are not enemies that work in opposition to each other but are constantly striving to stay in balance. As we can see, our fight-and-flight response is necessary for our very survival and like a pair of scales coming back into balance, our rest-and-digest system soothes our nerves when the danger is over. However, our modern way of living means there are influences in our lives that have the power to stimulate our fight-and-flight response on an ongoing basis. Unlike caveman, whose sympathetic nervous system would be in full flight as he puts his life in danger to hunt and kill for his lunch, to then enjoy some rest and repose during his afternoon nap; the delineation between fight-and-flight and rest-and-digest in a hectic, technology-driven, modern world is not so clear. Unfortunately, lifestyles that involve excessive stimulation and continual access to information and people through technology mean the balance of our scale is all too often tipped toward fight-and-flight.

It is said that a frog won't jump out of a pot of water as it gets hotter and hotter on a stove because it's unaware the water is heating up and it will stay there until it dies. We find ourselves in the same predicament as we live much of our lives with the sympathetic nervous system in an active state. A slow boil of worries and troubles, with little time to turn off, keeps us in a state of fight-and-flight. We are prone to plough on through the challenges of life, disconnected and unaware of the important signals our body sends that something is wrong.

Are you beginning to see why it's important to visit these intellectual, physical, and emotional aspects of yourself each day, and how much you could enjoy fostering your potential if you felt more control?

You see, your mind is a continual loop of information involving your thoughts, emotions, and body. If you tune into your physical body, it can tell you a lot about the state of your thoughts and emotions. Maybe you wake up in the morning with a sick feeling in your stomach, or you notice your heart racing when you're required to speak in public. Perhaps you go weak in the knees at the thought of entering a room full of strangers. These physical messages are all strong indications that you've dialled into unhelpful thoughts that are triggering your emotions.

It's common in our busy lives to become numb to the thoughts, emotions, and physical signals that indicate we are out of balance. Unconscious conversations that ruminate about the past or worry about the future causing knots in the stomach or raised blood pressure all become an everyday occurrence. We do everything we can to keep the symptoms at bay, which is a little like holding beach balls underwater, it's ineffective and very tiring.

Chapter 12
Spiritual Aspect

So, what's this spiritual aspect all about? Spirit comes from the Latin word for breath, "spiritus." In Sanskrit, Hebrew, and classical Chinese there are similar links between the words used for breath and spirit. Although everyone knows what breath means, the concept of spirituality can mean different things to different people. I was bought up as a Christian and as a child regularly went to church. I could see that my parents, along with many other people, drew enormous solace and meaning from their faith. But my spiritual connections were cemented early on, standing on that hillside in the Lake District with the rain on my face and the mud seeping around my boots. For me, a spiritual experience or getting in touch with the spiritual aspect of myself can happen anywhere, any time, and does not have to be tied to a religion. I can go to a church, temple, or synagogue, and experience the peace and energy of these places just as I can have a spiritual experience chanting in a yoga class, sitting in meditation, or standing quietly on a hillside with the sun on my face. If you've never thought about it before, it's useful to consider what the spiritual aspect of you is. Outside of religion, doctrine, or common descriptions, what is your spirit? Where is it and how do you experience it in your life?

Spirit to me is the non-physical, pure essence of a person. It appears intangible, and yet when we become more conscious and are in touch with this pure essence, we can feel at one with something much bigger than ourselves, outside of our comprehension and yet at the same time a completely integral part of who we are. At which point it seems a very natural and tangible thing. Deepak Chopra, author, and well-being pioneer says, "The deepest level of consciousness is spirit and spirit is pure potential." Spirit is the creative source of all of us.

Some people express spirit through art, writing, or painting, some through meaningful work that puts them in touch with their true nature of love and compassion. Others find it in prayer or meditation. Whenever we feel a sense of purpose in our lives and are in a state of allowing, trust, and receptivity, we are in touch with spirit. And why is this so important? Because that bulb of pure potential that was shining so brightly when you were born is full of your spirit, but it's been somewhat dimmed by the passage of time.

We all have moments of living out of this spirit potential, the trick is to have a life filled with more of these moments. Athletes call it being in the zone, and dancers know it as an experience of becoming one with the dance. Writers experience it when words seem to be effortlessly downloaded and poured onto the page, and artists create their best work from this timeless space.

How does this happen? In these moments all thought, emotional blockage, and physical disharmony cease to exist, and the mind-body machine becomes an uninterrupted vessel able to tap into pure potential. The athlete forgets all doubt and fear and glides effortlessly through the water or around the racetrack, the dancer feels fully embodied and trusts that every move will emerge exactly as desired. The writer is lost in time as the words flow without censorship, and the artist becomes one with the paint on the canvas or the clay in her hands as the creation emerges without trepidation or limitation.

In everyday life, the uninterrupted state of pure potential is when your intellectual, emotional, physical, and spiritual aspects are working in harmony. You spiral up, one aspect feeding the next, in a continual cycle of clarity, confidence, energy, and inspiration. You feel purposeful and life flows as you find yourself in the right place at the right time and whatever you need to progress comes to you. You don't have to be an artist or a dancer to have experienced these moments. We've all had them, however fleeting. You may have brushed them off as chance or luck, but no, that was you coming home to your potential. They are moments that feel natural and easy because they are. The trouble is you barely register them, or understand how they happen, let alone have any awareness that they happen because you are in tune with yourself and life. So, when life gets messy again, instead of tending to your inner world to restore equilibrium, you get action-oriented and look outside of yourself for your comfort or motivation, which is a short-term fix.

So why am I telling you all this? Because I wish someone had told me when I was in primary school that I would at times experience the gnawing, nervousness of butterflies in my tummy. I wish someone had explained to me that everyone feels nervous or stupid at times and that butterflies are normal. I wish I'd known as a teenager that I was accumulating and storing away thoughts and beliefs about the negative experiences of my life. It would have been useful to know that those unhelpful thoughts and beliefs were colouring my perception of myself and driving my behaviour. I wish someone had explained to me that my lack of confidence, feelings of inadequacy, doubts, fears, and false bravado were all generated by my mind. It would have been helpful to know that I would tend to measure myself and my success against others in an unfavourable way. I wish my school curriculum had included classes on how to manage the mind. It would have been inspiring if someone had taught me at a young age that how I think, feel, and act is completely my responsibility and totally within my control. And it would have been liberating to know that my enjoyment of life was not dependent on external events being a certain way, or people behaving how I want them to.

How much easier life would have been if I had known that my potential is intrinsically linked to the health of my intellectual, emotional, physical, and spiritual well-being, not simply my abilities or skills. And that the key to reaching more of my potential would not be found by changing who I am, but in getting to know and understand my inner self. Growing up would have been easier if my schooling had taught me that potential isn't something one person has, and another doesn't. And everything would have been more enjoyable if I had known that potential is an ever-moving feast, and the direction in which it moves is dependent on the state of my inner world and my mindset.

That you and you alone are responsible for the way you think, feel, and act might be hard to digest. It might be hard to stop believing that your mother-in-law isn't the cause of your annoyance, that your children are not the cause of your worry, or your ex the reason for your anger. The people in your workplace are not the cause of your frustration, and your happiness is not sapped by the people around you or dependent on your life being a certain way. I'm aware that this may come as bad news, not the least of which is that you have no one to blame but yourself for how you feel. Bummer, that's hard to take! So, if you're struggling with it, take it on board as a concept and as you work through the rest of this book and practice the exercises you will begin to see that it is so. Having no-one or no-thing to blame for your unhappiness may be tough, but it's also the greatest news you are ever going to receive because it puts you back in control of your life.

Having said I wish I'd known all these things at school, there's no silver bullet, no shortcuts, no magic moment when we suddenly become fully enlightened, and life is fine and dandy from that point on. It's a continual journey during which we are given opportunities to wake up to our true nature of pure potential. Or not.

Knowledge is power, and I hope that you'll take this knowledge on yourself and model it to the children in your life. I hope you can live with less resistance, anxiety, and self-doubt and instead experience life feeling resilient and excited at the prospect of discovering more and more of your potential.

PART III

Chapter 13
Airing Out Your House

I realise this is the part of the book where you might be wondering what's coming next. You may have flicked ahead and can see there's a segment with some practical exercises that I'm going to suggest you integrate into your life. You're seeking improvement or change, you wouldn't be reading this book otherwise, and I understand you may be a little upset if I suggest you rise each day before dawn and do some weird barefoot practice on the lawn. Plus, you're probably hoping these exercises can be done in the comfort of your home because you don't want your friends to think you've turned into a hippy. "And," I hear you say, "how on earth am I supposed to keep the intellectual, emotional, physical, and spiritual aspects of myself healthy; most days I barely have time to eat lunch!" Well, there goes your mind, chatting away again! And yes, our lives have become full and busy, and as wonderful as technology is, its reach into our lives means it's possible to be in a tiring state of stimulation for most of the day. Long gone are the days when we would work in rhythm with our body clock and the rise and fall of the sun. Unfortunately, when life gets frenetic, looking after our health and well-being is low on our list of priorities. And that's what makes me so dedicated to this work.

There's another reason I'm so dedicated to delivering this message. I don't want you to have to go through the steep learning curve that we did many years ago. A few years after we moved to Australia my husband woke up with a strong sense that something was more seriously wrong with him than his winter cold and cough. Only a few hours later we were sitting in the Oncology department at our local hospital. At the time, my husband was a fit, robust thirty-seven-year-old. We ate well, took our vitamins, and did plenty of exercise, how could this happen? I'm sure many of you know how frightening being diagnosed with a serious illness is. How your life changes in an instant and suddenly everything that seemed important the day before is forgotten, as you become consumed with the job of staying alive.

My husband was fortunate to have had a form of cancer, that with treatment, had a high recovery rate. But the months of chemotherapy with all the side effects that come with it were at times gruelling for him. Those of you who have been through anything similar, know that the ripple effect of fear and uncertainty also takes its toll on children, and loved ones. However hard and unwanted a situation may be, there is always something to be learned from it. The experience of caring for my husband through his cancer was the ultimate wake-up call. It confirmed to me that not just our physical health, but all aspects of a person must be attended to if we want to enjoy health and well-being. It also confirmed to me that managing the mind must be high on our list of priorities.

My husband made a full recovery, in fact, more than that, he only had half his conventional treatment before he went into full remission. How did he do that? I believe it was because he addressed the intellectual, emotional, physical, and spiritual aspects of well-being with vigour. He addressed the health of his mind and his body.

A healthy diet, regular exercise, and fresh air are a given for anyone wanting to remain in good health, and rest assured, I'm not going to tell you to sit cross-legged on the floor and meditate at four o'clock each morning, although please feel free if that appeals to you! But, the practices I am going to teach you will address your inner world and the role of the intimate mind-body connection that is so important to health and well-being. The practices are simple, practical, and profound, and can be easily integrated into your life. They will help you break free of negative ingrained thought patterns and unhelpful emotions and attitudes.

Remember, we have little to no control over what goes on outside of us, but we do have the capacity to care for our internal well-being and thus bring ourselves to the challenges we face in life firing on all cylinders. It's not going to be difficult, but it will take practice, patience, and persistence.

Let's begin!

Chapter 14
Step 1: Pay Attention

Airing out the Intellectual Aspect

The first thing we need to do is to *pay attention* to our thoughts! Apart from the obvious everyday thoughts of what to have for lunch or how to ask your boss for a raise, research shows we have thousands of unnoticed thoughts each day.

Then there are the findings of psychologist and economist Daniel Kahneman, who is notable for his work on the psychology of judgment and decision-making. He predicts that the psychological present, meaning moments of focus, is a window of about three seconds. Everything else we think is based in the past or the future.

Research at Harvard University by Daniel Gilbert and Matthew Killingsworth showed that out of more than two thousand responses, minds were wandering 46.9% of the time. This means that almost half of our lives are spent thinking of something other than what is going on in the present moment. And numerous cognitive neuroscientists have conducted studies revealing that only 3% of our cognitive activities, decisions, emotions, actions, behaviour, are conscious, meaning we are fully aware and alert to them. The remaining 97% is generated automatically or unconsciously.

We've talked about the backpack of memories and life experiences we all carry around; it's this information that informs our unconscious thoughts, beliefs, habits, and emotions. This is the part of our mind that's on automatic pilot and churns out the same repetitive thoughts each day. We're not aware that these thoughts are operating but they quietly speak to us and inform our behaviour all day, every day. No conscious thought process is at work here, hence why it's called the unconscious mind, and when living in this unconscious way we miss many of the very precious moments of our lives.

The research stating that of the thousands of thoughts we have per day, 80% have a negative quality to them and 95% are the same thoughts as the previous day comes from a 2005 study by the National Science Foundation. Taking these pieces of research into account, it's safe to say that we are spending an awful lot of energy processing random thoughts that are unhelpful and rarely applicable to the reality of what we are experiencing in the present moment. When we do manage to activate our conscious mind and be present, our ability to enjoy those precious moments lasts for an average of three seconds!

How many times have you arrived home from a regular journey you take; perhaps from work, either in your car or on a train or bus, and as you put your key in the door you realise you have very little recollection of your journey home. I'm sure you've also had the experience of not taking in someone's name when being introduced. These are classic examples of our tendency to be distracted and our limited capacity to be psychologically present.

Next time you're on a crowded street, in a restaurant, or on a train look around you and consider that many of the people you see aren't fully there; their minds have taken them somewhere else, and very often somewhere unhelpful! On a more serious note, the life experience we miss because of our inability to harness the mind is tragic. We miss taking in the richness of precious events, we miss enjoying the fullness of our children, the connection of our relationships, the depth of our loved ones, and the wonder of life.

In a moment you're going to begin the process of learning how to gain some control over your rather reckless mind. It's important to remember as you move into exploring the different aspects of yourself that they are intricately connected, and though one or two aspects may be more dominant, one is never active without the others. We'll explore these aspects starting with the intellect, and then move on to investigate how intellectual thought impacts emotions and the physical body. However, as you become more deeply acquainted with your mind and body, you'll recognise that it's often the emotional or the physical aspects that tell you when something is wrong. We can identify the more overt indications of imbalance, such as a knot in the stomach or a feeling of nausea, anger, or sadness quite easily. However, our thoughts and beliefs are harder to pinpoint in moments of disturbance. So, it would make sense to become attuned to these stronger indications that we are out of balance, provided by the emotional and physical aspects of ourselves, so we can correct these imbalances as quickly as possible.

The skill of becoming acquainted with your internal dialogue is a useful tool. It's also important to know that a belief is simply a thought that you've had over and again. My belief that I'm hopeless at maths is only there because I've had that thought so many times, not only when a situation has arisen to remind me but also unconsciously without my awareness. The process that I'm going to show you next is not something you need to do every time you're upset. The beauty of healing yourself using this form of self-inquiry is that there is no need to dredge up any suffering from the past and intellectually analyse it or try to understand it. Any thoughts that trigger emotion and physical reaction in the body come mostly from our unconscious mind, but it's impossible to change the unconscious mind just by thinking.

To try and intellectually scrutinise your unconscious is futile. The unconscious mind is like a record player; the song will not change until you change the record, which is best done by investigating your emotions and the physical reactions these emotions cause. However, it's enlightening to know how far-reaching our untamed and unchecked mind chatter can go, and when you see how unhelpful the conversations are that you regularly have with yourself, you'll hopefully be inspired to take back control.

I think we've established by now that it's our mind rather than the external circumstances of our lives that make us feel so hopeless at times. I want to be clear here, I'm not condoning bad behaviour. If you've experienced trauma and upset because of life circumstances or other people's cruel actions, that should not have happened to you and I'm truly sorry for that. And the only person who can make you feel better about yourself and your life is you. There are great short-term coping mechanisms that will help you get by and feel better for a while, but if you want long-lasting, positive change, investigating how your mind works and how to make it your best friend will set you up for life.

When we learn to *pay attention* to our thoughts and become aware that our mind chatter is fuelling our negative emotions, we can come back to the present moment reality of what is going on externally and internally. When we have this awareness, we have control and can respond to situations with calm composure rather than letting our habitual reactions take over.

Are you still resenting something long past, continually agonising about your kids, fretting over what a work colleague said to you last week, or worrying about something in the future? Next time you're agitated, angry, anxious, or when any negative emotion is present, *pay attention* to your thoughts and remind yourself that your thoughts are fuelling those feelings.

Let's explore this some more

If you're not convinced you have these conversations going on, try this revealing exercise that I call a Thought Cascade. First, identify the incident that has activated the negative emotions you're feeling. Next, write down the feelings and emotions you're experiencing. Be very honest about what you are thinking and believing about this incident. What is your mind saying? I suggest as you go through this exercise you close your eyes, tune into that inner voice, and listen carefully. Now it's your turn.

Exercise 3 - Thought Cascade

Incident - Write down the event or occasion that has caused your upset. Try to identify the moment you became triggered. If it was an interaction with someone, when was the precise moment you became upset; if it was something you saw, heard, or experienced, when was the exact moment that event affected you?

For example - *My partner spends all his spare time with his friends or in his man cave. Yesterday I went out to where he was fixing his car and gave him a cup of tea and he didn't even stop what he was doing to acknowledge me. The exact moment I became upset was as I put the cup down on the bench and realised he wasn't going to come out from under the car.*

Feeling – Write down how this incident leaves you feeling. What emotions are you experiencing, and what physical sensations are you feeling in your body?

For example - *It makes me feel angry, sad, and lonely; I feel unloved.*

Mind Chatter – Write down all the thoughts and beliefs being generated by the conversations you are having in your head about this incident. Listen carefully and write everything down, from the trivial to the shocking. Be honest about any blaming, shaming, catastrophising, self-criticism, or plotting revenge. Get it all out on paper.

For example - *He'll never change, he's not capable of affection, our marriage is a sham, I'm wasting my life in this relationship, other couples don't treat each other with such disrespect, he's going to leave me, I'll be all alone, it's not fair, maybe I should put my foot down.*

Here are some more examples

- *My team are not reaching their targets at work. I noticed a wave of anxiety come over me when Julie was going through the financial forecast in this morning's meeting.*
- *I feel sick to my stomach, distracted, nervous, and exhausted.*
- *My blood pressure is going to go up again, I can't do anything to motivate my team, I'll lose my job, I'll have no money, my family will fall apart. No one appreciates me there anyway. Stuff it, maybe I should just leave, I'm too good for that place anyway.*

Or

- *My teenagers are out socialising and won't do their homework. The moment I realised I felt so stressed about this was when one of the Mums at school told me how hard her daughter was studying for her exams.*
- *I feel anxious and have a constant knot in my chest, I feel nervous all the time and I can't sleep properly.*
- *My relationship with my kids will get worse because they think I'm nagging them all the time. They'll fail their exams, they'll have extremely limited choices in life, be dependent on me, and have unhappy and unfulfilling lives.*

Or

- *My partner is constantly working, watching television or sleeping and doesn't seem interested in me at all.*
- *I feel unappreciated, I'm tired of trying so hard, I'm constantly disappointed by our interactions and angry about this behaviour.*
- *I feel like the people at work are more important than me. I'm bottom of the pile, nothing I do is good enough, I'm supportive in every way I can be, and this is how I'm treated. Our relationship is failing, I should find someone who appreciates me.*

Even though we're exploring the intellectual aspect in this section, as you can see this process also uncovers the emotions and feelings. You'll notice the process asks you to identify the emotions and physical sensations in your body before listening to the mind chatter. In other words, the emotional and physical aspects are being investigated first. This is because every thought we have stimulates an emotion that is felt as a physical sensation somewhere in the body, and it's usually the physical sensations in the body that will alert us to the fact that something is wrong. What we feel in the body is far more obvious to us than the more subtle realms of thought and emotion. When we are under pressure, we'll know our palms are sweating or our heart is racing before we can identify exactly what thoughts and emotions are triggering these symptoms. We'll feel a nauseous churning in our stomach before we understand the thoughts that have triggered it. For now, we're going to investigate each of these aspects individually, and as you become acquainted with your habits around thoughts, emotions, and physical sensations, you'll see how this incredible, intricate mind-body communication network interacts.

At this stage, we are concerned with identifying the mind chatter and becoming familiar with the conversations you're having in your head. These are the thoughts and beliefs sitting in the unconscious mind, the ones that are not consciously heard but whisper in your ear and play an enormous part in how you feel about yourself, others, and life. When you learn to tune into the feelings in your body and the messages they are sending, and you become more conscious in moments of upset, you become aware that the mind is playing tricks on you. Soon you'll learn to quickly come back to the present moment and to the truth of what is going on. This is how you gain real control.

What do you notice about your mind chatter? Do you see that when we have these conversations in our head about challenging situations, or just stuff and nonsense, they are full of future predictions or past regrets? The content of these unconscious conversations can seem confusing and convoluted, but at their foundation, they are quite simple. These inner conversations only ever involve you, someone, or something else, and will have their roots in future predictions or past ruminations. That's it. In a nutshell, we spend most of our time chatting away to ourselves about our involvement in a situation that may also involve others from the standpoint of an illusory past or an imagined future.

The reason these conversations trigger our emotions and cause physical symptoms such as a churning stomach or a pounding heart is that the mind is so much more than just the brain. The body has no idea whether what you are thinking is true or not. Remember we talked earlier about the sympathetic nervous system being responsible for your body's rapid involuntary response to threatening or stressful situations? When you imagine (which is what you are doing, because as we've identified these thoughts are based in the past or the future, so they can only be imagined) that your child is going to fail their exams or you're going to lose your job, your whole system is charged, ready to take on the threat. The threat is not real, it's imagined, but your body doesn't know that. And if you do lose our job the mind will continue to create all manner of stories about that, how you'll lose your home, your family, your dignity, and on and on this catastrophic mind chatter goes!

Can you see that the physical symptoms you experience, such as tension in your shoulders, a knot in your chest, or feeling sick to your stomach, can be due to the emotions you're experiencing that are triggered by the imagined thoughts you're having? We'll talk more about emotions and physical symptoms later because that's where we get our real information and deep healing. But it's important and useful to understand our thought processes as well.

If you want to feel happier, more at peace, and in control of your life, it will serve you well to stop blaming the events of your life for your unhappiness, and instead, investigate what you are believing about those events. Because that's where your unhappiness comes from, your thoughts, not the events themselves. And if you already know this, I urge you to become even more astute, tune in even more deeply. Are you feeling a bit gloomy or unsettled, do you feel frustrated with your partner or children, or do you doubt your ability at work? As you journey on your road through life, every emotion is a signpost that can point you back to investigate the truth of your thoughts, which is the first step to gaining control of your experience. As my old friend William Shakespeare said in his play Hamlet, "There is nothing either good or bad, but thinking makes it so."

As you become more adept at paying attention to your thoughts, you'll notice that you can categorise your mind chatter into two camps. The first type of mind chatter is the thoughts and beliefs we've just explored in the Thought Cascade. We don't easily notice this mind chatter. Sure, we feel upset or angry, but we rarely take the time to identify the deeper reason for our emotions, which is why it's useful to write it down. These thoughts can be confusing, full of sentiment and physical symptoms, and for them to dissipate, they need to be proactively addressed with understanding and self-compassion. We'll discuss how to do this in the coming chapters.

The second type of mind chatter is more like a loud, monotonous conversation that's usually about something quite trivial, and with a little practice and a clear intention, can be banished quite quickly by simply telling it to STOP! Let me give you an example of both within one story.

A friend of mine who's divorced was due to attend her daughter's wedding where her ex-husband and his new, young wife would also be in attendance. In the lead-up to the wedding, she noticed that she was feeling nervous about the event, and old resentments towards her ex-husband were re-surfacing. So, she knew it was time to explore her deeper mind chatter. She spent some time identifying the unhelpful thoughts and beliefs that were being triggered by this event. Her imaginings about the wedding and ruminations about her past relationship were causing her unrest, and she knew her sense of self-worth had taken a battering because of these thoughts. By the time the wedding day arrived she was feeling more confident and self-assured and felt she'd put herself in the best possible frame of mind to enjoy the day and let the past be the past.

All was well until her ex-husband arrived and took centre stage in the church with his new wife. This is when she identified the second type of mind chatter, the trivial, monotonous conversation, which in her case was all about how crazy her ex was to marry someone so young; you get the gist! But, because my friend is a wise woman and works proactively to take charge of her mind, she was able to catch herself and instruct her mind chatter to stop. She knew she was distracted and had fallen into the category of almost half of people whose mind is somewhere other than where they are in the present moment. She realised that she'd been "hooked" by her mind and was focussed on the futile conversation in her head, rather than the especially important scene before her, the marriage of her daughter. And lucky she did, because she was about to miss one of the most precious moments of her daughter's life. So, what did she do? She told herself to "STOP!" She became conscious and intentional about how she wanted to be and feel from that moment on. Then she was able to immerse herself in the joy of her daughter's wedding without the distraction of disruptive mind chatter. This came about because she was paying attention.

You'll know the thoughts that need extra investigation. These are the inner conversations that trigger your emotions and cause physical discomfort in your body. And then there are the monotonous conversations that you can simply instruct to stop. Next time you know you're thinking something that's mean, unhelpful, laced with resentment, or just downright ridiculous, *pay attention* and stop it. If you're rehearsing an angry conversation in your head that you'll have with your co-worker who's offended you, stop it. If you're looking in the mirror and having a conversation with yourself about everything that's aging on your face, stop it. If you're stewing over a disagreement you've had with your partner and finding all their faults, stop it. If you're doing the washing-up at midnight and complaining to yourself that everyone takes you for granted, simply stop, not the washing up, the conversation in your head! If you're moaning in your mind because your neighbours have gone on another holiday, and you haven't had a holiday for years… Stop it.

I'm not condoning bad behaviour and it may be that you need to have a conversation with your work colleague who offended you, or your partner who never does the dishes. But can you see how this type of habitual, unconscious, internal dialogue is never going to contribute in any meaningful way to the resolution of the problem, let alone to your well-being or happiness?

When we become more aware of our limiting behaviour and take responsibility for it, we learn to respond to external circumstances rather than react to them. When I have a deadline looming, as I do with this book, and I start feeling anxious, I know immediately that I'm blowing things out of proportion, believing I don't have enough time, and imagining whatever needs doing is out of my control or capability. This is when I say to myself "stop" and as soon as I do, I get a much clearer perspective and can find a solution. Start today, see if you can begin to identify the unhelpful conversations you have with yourself, and instruct them to stop.

To be clear, I'm not telling you to stop thinking. I'm not sure if you've ever tried to stop thinking but go ahead and give it a try, it's not easy. But we can instruct our mind to cease from a specific negative thought process that is gathering momentum. Because when our thoughts gain momentum, day after day, over and again, they become beliefs. Just like the thought I had over and again throughout my life that I'm hopeless at maths, that eventually became a belief I had about myself. This process of paying attention to thought is like spring cleaning the intellectual aspect of your mind. This contributes to your whole mind-body system being able to operate with more ease, control, and composure, which in turn boosts your health and well-being. More to come on that later.

There are more practices in the coming chapters, and once we've investigated the emotional, physical, and spiritual aspects, you'll understand that this intricate and sophisticated web that is the mind-body can be harnessed, giving you a more embodied, internal sense of control in your life. Ask yourself whether you're happy with the idea that unchecked conversations are going on in your head, the likes of which you would never have if you knew how damaging they were to your confidence, self-worth, happiness, and success. For now, the first lesson in this Intellectual Aspect is to *PAY ATTENTION.*

Chapter 15

Step 2: Embrace and Explore

Airing out the Emotional and Physical Aspect

The reason we're going to explore the emotional and physical aspects together is that as you become more attuned to your mind and body, you'll notice the undeniable link between your emotions, and the physical sensations they ignite in your body.

What we will do here, is a gentle exploration into the emotional and physical aspects of you. This will help you understand the chain of events that can be set off by one simple thought. You'll begin to identify some habits you may have formed that are not supporting your well-being or happiness.

Depending on the situation, emotions and physical sensations can be subtle or strong. Of course, we humans come in all shapes and sizes, with differing personalities. Some of you are very in touch with your emotions; in fact, they can be the very thing that informs the decisions you make in life. More women than men fall into this category, and if this is you what we're going to discuss in this chapter will resonate clearly with you. Other women are more analytical, and process things via logic and data, if that's you, the very word "emotion" may put you off reading further. Let me reassure you, this exploration into emotions is gentle, and driven by you, so you are always in control. It's simply an opportunity for you to explore the sometimes subtle, and sometimes overt link between your thoughts, your emotions, and the feelings they evoke in your body.

Why would we do this? Well, as we've already identified, your emotions, and the sensations they produce in your body, are caused by your unhelpful thoughts. But you can't think your way out of your mind. You can certainly work logically through something that's bothering you, take some deep breaths, and plan what action you're going to take to remedy the situation. But if the emotion around this bothersome event lingers, these short-term fixes will never enable it to fully dissipate.

However, exploring the physical expression of an emotion instigates an innate and miraculous process of dissolving the negative emotion, and can even bring clarity and understanding to confusing thoughts.

Our emotions are constantly triggered, as we process the myriad of events we experience in the world around us. We are touched by a story we read in the newspaper, we feel sad for a friend who's lost a loved one, we get frustrated that we couldn't complete a task, or confused by a throwaway comment. We can feel drained by our workload or get angry when we're exhausted or our children are being loud and boisterous. Some people can identify strongly with the emotions they feel moment to moment, while other people are not so aware of them. There is no right or wrong, we're all different, and have a preference as to whether we process things intellectually or emotionally.

Western society, unlike many eastern cultures, often conditions us to pay more heed to the head than the heart. Certain cultures are more emotionally driven than others. Spain and Italy are emotional cultures, where people are more open and expressive; whereas England, Australia, and the USA are more intellectual cultures where people tend to be more guarded emotionally. Another important distinction to make is the difference between being emotional, and emotional intelligence. Emotionally preferenced people can be more demonstrative and open with their emotions, but in this context, we are talking about it being a fundamental driver and information provider. Emotionally intelligent people tend to make decisions more from their hearts than from their heads. Although they obviously take in data and think logically, it's the subtle realm of the emotional body that feeds them the clearest information and drives their decisions. This can be difficult for those who operate from their intellect to comprehend, just as it can be challenging for emotionally intelligent people to live in a world dominated by intellectually preferenced people.

Emotional intelligence is supported by self-awareness, as emotions can be deep in our psyche. Psychologist Daniel Goleman describes it beautifully in his best-selling book *Emotional Intelligence* as "knowing one's internal states, preference, resources and intuitions." This intelligence is slowly being recognised for the immense importance it has in our world. Intellectual intelligence is important of course, but it's dominated the western world to the detriment of our ability to connect with ourselves, others, and nature. Some of the practices you'll learn later will open you to more of your emotional intelligence.

The key here is to meet emotions just as they are, rather than to push them away or ignore them. When you experience emotions and feelings that are unhelpful, such as fear, resentment, anger, guilt, or shame, your ability to *embrace and explore* them, and their physical expression is what will help you move through them. We tend to believe that we must crush negative emotions to get rid of them, when in fact the opposite is true. Your capacity to be with any emotion will allow you the freedom to enjoy more regularly feeling calm, peaceful, and at ease. It's an important step towards being able to witness the emotions you have rather than getting entrapped by them and allowing them to randomly dominate your experience of life. More on witnessing later.

I remember very clearly when I first experienced the power of simply allowing emotions and feelings to be present, as a way to move beyond them. As I've mentioned, for much of my life I've been a meditator, and I've also had a lot of education and experience coaching and mentoring people. I'd spent many hours being trained to unearth negative mind chatter and to breathe away or let go of negative emotions. This is certainly useful and better than wallowing in them, but I soon discovered that what I needed to let go of was my resistance to experiencing negative emotions. Pushing them away or ignoring them is like a band-aid, the wound is still festering underneath.

The process, taught to me by Dr. Richard Miller the founder of the iRest Institute, surpassed all this by far. The iRest Institute is an educational non-profit that trains teachers in the healing benefits of yogic and meditative practices. Dr. Miller is someone I feel truly blessed to have met because his teachings have had such a positive influence on my life, and my work. He calls the process of allowing feelings and emotions to be present "welcoming" and it was under his guidance that I began to experience truly welcoming my emotions and exploring their physical expression as a path to relief from suffering.

By the time I did my iRest teacher training in 2013, I'd practiced meditation for many years, but I'm extremely glad I took the opportunity to learn more, even though I got off to a rocky start. I'd booked myself in for the week-long teacher training, knowing it would be good for me to expose myself to another practice. But when the time arrived, I was inundated with work and couldn't see how it would be possible to take a whole week off to attend the training. As I tried to organise myself around this week-long training I was undertaking, I was kicking myself for signing up. I drove to the training centre just outside Melbourne feeling distracted and disengaged. Even the beautiful tranquil setting and energy of the venue did little to soothe my agitation.

The large training room was set on the second level of the building with big windows looking out to the Australian bush. There were about twenty people in the course, and we settled in with notebooks at the ready. Telling myself I should make the most of the course, I tried to forget the things that were on my mind and after hastily messaging instructions to work colleagues I turned off my phone. The training was immediately interesting, and I began to relax, feeling happier about my decision to attend, even though I was still distracted by my commitments at work. I sat on my yoga mat bolstered by cushions and blankets and was guided into deep relaxation. Then we were invited to notice the different feelings and emotions that were coming and going in our experience. I had plenty to explore, I was worried about some printing I needed to get done for a workshop I was running the following week, and double-checking in my mind that I'd informed all my clients that daytime classes were cancelled. I was also fretting about travelling home in rush-hour traffic in time to teach an evening yoga class.

Through expert and gentle instruction, I could quickly identify a buzz of frenetic energy in my body and a slight churning in my stomach. The link between my thoughts about my work and the physical sensations these thoughts were causing in my body was palpable. This process was familiar to me, and something I had been trained to identify and work with as a self-esteem coach. But then something happened that I'd not experienced before. I was instructed to welcome my emotions and the physical sensations they caused in my body, just as they were. As if by magic everything changed, it was as if my whole system were being validated, rather than just my brain. I experienced a sense of powerful inner control and peace that hadn't seemed possible a few moments before. My concerns about my work and clients began to dissipate as I changed my relationship with these unwanted emotions and feelings by allowing them to be there. My mind became clear, my body relaxed, and I felt a strong sense of inner composure. As the full impact of what had just happened hit me, I almost leaped to my feet with excitement. I had spent years meditating, trying not to pay my thoughts any attention by keeping my focus on my breath or various other focal techniques. I'd spent a great deal of my life learning how to process difficult beliefs and emotions through written or spoken practices. These processes provided some clarity and short-term relief, but nothing came close to the depth of resolution this simple practice provided. Exploring my emotions and feelings in a spirit of curiosity and acceptance, and with no need to work things out, enabled my mind and body to settle back into a state of balance and self-control with ease. From that moment on I was fully engaged and delighted with my choice to embark on the teacher training. Since that time, I've taken hundreds of clients through this process, enabling them to find relief from fear, pain, lack of confidence, anxiety, self-doubt, and a myriad of other human challenges. The iRest Institute has now trained thousands of teachers all over the world.

Just as I did, you can begin to hone this skill right away by simply being more alert to your thoughts and feelings, exploring them with curiosity rather than trying to ignore or manipulate them. Emotions are like a small child pulling at your trouser leg and pleading for your attention. Anyone who's experienced a child doing this knows they don't give up easily! When you ignore them, they'll persist even more, just like your emotions. But when you turn to that child and give her the attention she wants, the pulling at the trouser leg stops.

When you learn to *embrace* and *explore* your thoughts, emotions, and feelings, you begin to cultivate one of the most significant parts of a yoga practice, which is to witness one's mind. When you can integrate this practice of observation in your life and watch the flow of your mind, you'll be more likely to have a useful and compassionate conversation with yourself that says something like, "I'm noticing my anger." Or "I'm aware I'm feeling frustrated," rather than the usual unconscious conversation of blaming and shaming which sounds something like, "boy, he makes me angry," or "I'm such an idiot, why did I do that?" You have a unique ability to develop this deeper layer of awareness that exists alongside the sensory, emotional, and conceptual experiences you have.

You see, there's always the experience you're having, and then there's your awareness or recognition of it. Being more attentive to the quality of your thoughts, and meeting your emotions creates a natural pause during which you can calmly watch yourself in the experience. Rather than the common habit of paying no attention to your thoughts, blaming outside events for your upset, and allowing yourself to become submerged in your emotions. All the while believing you have no option but to feel this way. Can you sense the power this simple change of focus gives you to respond rather than react to events?

This liberating step of *embracing and exploring* emotions and feelings enables us to quickly put into perspective what can appear to be very confusing when we let emotions take hold. It's simply a matter of becoming more conscious, and we become more conscious through the process of meditation.

Every emotion we experience instigates a series of physiological reactions that can often be felt in the body. In my personal experience and in working with many clients, it appears we all have our favourites. Mine tends to be churning in my stomach when I'm nervous, frenzied energy in my body when life is hectic or I'm running late, and a knot in my chest when I'm upset. Let me give you an example of how this appears.

After I had children, I developed a fear of heights. I'd done many things in my life that involved heights before our children were born, and as a child, my favourite thing to do was climb up anything that took me higher. I'd been on ski lifts, rock-climbing walls, roller coasters, and perched on the edge of mountains without any problem. Then suddenly I found myself crippled with anxiety whenever we were anywhere high with our boys.

The first time it happened was on the top of a mountain here in the Victorian high country, an area that features a national park, lakes, snow resorts, and vineyards. It was spring and my family and I were enjoying a beautiful sunny day and a bright blue sky. We'd had an uneventful climb, stopping along the way to take in the magnificent rolling hills, covered in every shade of green bushland and stretching as far as the eye could see. We hardly saw any people on the way and the boys, although small, had lots of energy as we trudged up the track crunching dry leaves and twigs underfoot. As we reached the top, I was feeling very content and happy, until one of the boys noticed that there was still some height to be gained by climbing up an extra bit of rock. That was it, two young boys were not going to be satisfied until they reached the very top. It was an easy climb up a series of steps carved out of boulders onto the flat worn surface of the rock, but soon I found myself looking down a sheer drop on the other side with very little space to move around. The boys were elated, jumping for joy at their achievement, and thrilled by the amazing view. I, on the other hand, was terrified and my body had gone from feeling nicely tired and relaxed to a shaking, adrenaline-pumping mess within moments.

Of course, I was concerned for the boy's safety, but I was also confused as to why someone like me, who'd never felt afraid of heights before, had been possessed by this raging fear. I felt sick and my heart was racing, all of which seemed completely out of my control. I later had a similar reaction when we were on a chair lift, then another on a treetop walk, and roller-coaster rides were now off my agenda! Of course, these situations had a small element of danger, but the real cause of my anxiety came from my mind playing out some awful scenario in which my children's lives were at risk. These catastrophic thoughts and fearful emotions then set off a series of physical sensations in my body. Little did I know that our younger son was going to grow into an adventure-seeking, freedom-loving adrenaline junkie, so I've been given ample opportunity over the years to practice managing my anxiety!

I've learned to *pay attention* to my thoughts and stay focused on the reality of what's happening rather than buying into a scenario that could so easily be played out in my head. Often the reality of what's happening isn't what we'd choose. Watching my son jump off high clifftops into the ocean or do backflips on his snowboard makes me nervous, and that nervousness can escalate quickly if I allow my imagination to kick in. So, I've learned to be present and live in the moment, as they say, because living in an imagined future can be far worse.

The thing is the body doesn't know whether what we are experiencing is real or illusory. As I became more and more concerned about my children's safety on top of that mountain, my body began reacting to the unconscious thoughts I was having at the possibility of one of them falling off the cliff. Because I continued to let my thoughts run like a movie in my mind, my emotional body was triggered, and I felt real fear. Next, physical symptoms joined in, making me feel weak at the knees. This was, of course, the sympathetic nervous system in action. I sensed danger and my body responded. The problem is when we don't have some control over this intricate and brilliant process of protection and let our system know that it can stand down, it can become a habitual cycle. It's perfectly understandable how you might believe you have no control over your emotions, that they just come over you in waves completely uninvited. But you see, we do invite them in. We invite them in through the mind.

I encourage you to start turning your attention inward instead of outward and be more curious about what is triggering your emotions in your everyday life. When you find yourself feeling out of your depth, embarrassed, or tongue-tied, turn your attention inward, be curious about your thoughts and emotions, and explore the feelings in your body. When you're angry or frustrated, or someone's annoying you, instead of focusing your anger toward them, turn your attention inward and see what thoughts are triggering your anger. When you're stomping around the house, banging doors, or feeling belligerent, look within rather than trying to fix or blame external circumstances. When you find yourself withdrawing your attention or affection, be curious about why you feel that way. When you're afraid, turn your attention inward and get acquainted with your thoughts, emotions, and feelings.

We invite all emotions and physical symptoms into our experience via our thoughts. Sure, there are things in life we would rather not experience. But when we think it's only the situation or event that's making us upset, we've lost all power and control. Before that liberating day in my meditation teacher-training course, I'd been exposed to a lot of processes that enabled me to identify negative or unhelpful mind chatter. This is useful, but this gentle inner focus on my emotions and feelings was the missing piece that put me in the driver's seat.

You can't think your way out of your mind. You can try and make sense of things, and that makes you feel better for a while, but the emotions and feelings in the body have to be recognised and accepted for real healing to take place. Through the simple act of allowing emotions and feelings to be seen and felt, and exploring them with curiosity rather than judgment, they will start to dissipate. As I sat in my meditation teacher training all those years ago feeling lighter and more peaceful and composed than I had in years, I remember thinking, *why on earth would I continue to try and suppress or ignore my emotions and feelings, when they provide the gateway to freedom and control?*

Let's play with this some more

To experience this for yourself, read through these instructions, and then close your eyes and take yourself through this process.

In a moment I'm going to ask you to recall an event that is currently happening in your life that's causing you some angst. Think clearly about this event and notice the conversation you're having in your head about it. Then *embrace* the emotions that this recollection activates, simply as something that you're curious about without judgment. Then, you're going to identify the feelings that are present in your body due to this emotion. Here we go . . .

Exercise 4 – Tuning in to Thoughts, Emotions, and Sensations

1) The first step is to *pay attention* to the thoughts and conversations that we have with ourselves. Begin by identifying a situation in your life that you're finding challenging. What's going on in your life currently that frustrates you, who or what is annoying you, what's making you anxious, who's upset you, or what life situation are you worried about? Think about your work, your family, your friends, your community, or the wider world. What, or who is pushing your buttons? Do you notice that when you think about this situation in a more focussed and mindful way you can begin to hear the conversation you're having about it in your head? "I wish he would just ..." "She never listens..." "Why is it always me that has to...?" "They just don't understand..." "I wish I could..." "I'll never be able to..." "What is the world coming to...?"

   You'll notice that you get some clear mind chatter coming through when you focus on this situation that's causing you angst. Your mind will project forward into the future and play out how you think it's going to turn out or relive the past and churn it over. All of this happens in an instant.

2) Next, is the process of *embracing* your emotions. See if you can identify the emotion that comes with the story. Are you angry, sad, regretful, confused, disgusted, anxious, frustrated, guilty; what's the emotion you're experiencing? It's not necessary to precisely name it, it may be a mixture of different emotions, just tune into the emotional turmoil that is present because of this situation you're thinking about.

3) Now begin to *explore* your body and find the physical feeling that's happening because of this emotion. If you've never done this before, or if you're a person who rarely pays any heed to feelings of discomfort in your body, this will be a new experience for you. But give it a try. Can you locate the sensation that is stimulated in your body as you allow your thoughts to rouse your emotions? Close your eyes and see what's there. It might be very subtle, or it may be obvious and even familiar. It might be a knot in your chest or a tightness in your jaw, or a nervous feeling in your stomach. All emotions live somewhere in the body, your only job is to be curious and see what's there. Let everything be there just as it is. Continue to breathe, *embrace and explore* without any agenda to change anything.

Let your thoughts, emotions, and feelings be heard, seen, and felt without any agenda to fix or change them. Doing this is a very powerful expression of self-compassion.

It appears there's an element of losing control when we do this inner enquiry into our emotions and feelings because we are used to dealing with challenges in a more gritty and strong-minded way. We are conditioned to think that this is how we relieve pain, but it's only giving us the illusion that we are improving our situation. This gentle inner exploration enables us to move beyond our challenging thoughts and emotions and gives us back real control. Later, I'm going to explain how you can take this process further, enabling the emotional turmoil to settle, but for now experiment with *paying attention, embracing, and exploring.*

When we don't take a more mindful approach to disharmony in our lives, we tend to deal with life's challenges in the only way we know. We can become inflexible and stubborn, positioning ourselves as better, right, stronger, more intelligent, or more capable; or indeed by diminishing ourselves as stupid, incapable, guilty, ashamed, or a myriad of other beliefs we dredge up. This will always put us in a state of resistance rather than acceptance, and reaction rather than response. But, when we take responsibility for our discomfort and gently enquire into the reality of our personal, moment-by-moment experience, we can use this innate ability to understand our emotions and physical reactions and gain an enormous amount of inner control. When we live with more inner control it informs our decisions and actions and enables us to engage our full potential in a far more creative and productive way.

The key here is to change the habit that we formed growing up of believing our happiness will only come when our outer circumstances improve. Or, once we gain approval from the people we deem important in our lives. All the time, we were looking for solutions outside of ourselves to ease our discomfort instead of going within, where the real control lies. When we do go within, we access our intrinsic ability to take control of the way we think, feel, and act by becoming more self-aware. We find we can respond to any challenges, fears, self-doubt, and insecurity with calm, clear, composure rather than reacting out of our conditioning and unconscious habits.

For now, we are at the exploratory stage. Action through knowledge is power, so the process of paying more attention to the workings of your mind and engaging more openly with your emotions is useful. Later I'm going to give you some practices that will assist you to dissipate unhelpful emotions, release resistance, and help make this journey of inner control second nature to you. Not only because it's a much more pleasant, productive, and connecting way of engaging with life, but because it is far better for your health.

Scientists are now measuring what Yogis have known anecdotally for centuries, that the quality of our thoughts has a direct effect on our health. Allowing the mind to spend time engaged with thoughts that cause worry and anxiety means we spend a lot of time with our sympathetic nervous system (fight-or-flight response) in an active state. This is very demanding on the physical body, and when we continue to operate on this slow boil year after year, our health can be severely compromised.

Psychoneuroimmunology is a relatively new field of study and research into the understanding of the mind-body connection. As the name would suggest, PNI studies the relationship between psychological processes, the nervous system, and the immune system. Neurotransmitters control nearly all the body's functions, and our thoughts influence our body directly because the body will interpret the messages coming from the brain to prepare us for what's expected. It has become clear that if stress is not managed it can contribute to many health problems, such as heart disease and high blood pressure.

In a nutshell, grief, pain, anxiety, and distress throw you off balance. Also, simple life occurrences, and habitual negative attitudes such as the stress you feel when you're running late, or the upset you experience when you've argued, the negativity you feel from your boss, or the worry you engage in about your children or finances, all upset the body's delicate hormone balance. This not only depletes the brain chemicals required for happiness but also puts the immune system under pressure.

This is the reason stress management has become so popular because research now confirms that chronic stress, which means any stress that is frequent, prolonged, habitual, or persistent, is damaging to your health. When we live mindlessly with our unchecked negative thoughts and feelings running rampant and causing anxiety, the body is affected. But, by being more aware of our thoughts, emotions, and feelings, we can identify when we're off balance. Furthermore, if we engage in proactive daily routines and practices that keep us tuned to our parasympathetic nervous system, high-energy functions are slowed, and the body can regenerate in this balanced state of rest.

Bruce Lipton, American biologist, and author of the book *Biology of Belief* says it very succinctly. "The moment you change your perception is the moment you rewrite the chemistry of your body." In other words, the moment you *pay attention* and recognise that you're ruminating about something, and you *embrace* the emotion of that moment and *explore* the physical feelings it's causing, is the moment you have a choice. You can continue with a habitual pattern of unchecked thoughts and worry that will degenerate your body, or go within and gain control of your thoughts and emotions, which soothes your nervous system and rewrites the chemistry of your body. With practice, this can become second nature to you.

This chart will help you put into context what happens to the body when these different parts of the nervous system are stimulated.

Fight or Flight – think of putting your foot on the accelerator in your car	**Rest and Repose – think of gently pressing your foot on the brake**
Accelerator Yang Stress hormones released Raised heart rate Muscles contract Saliva production reduced Inhibits many of the functions of digestion Raised blood pressure Increased respiratory rate Sweating Body working hard and aging fast	Brake Yin Hormones in balance Heart rate drops Muscles relax Saliva production normal Digestive enzymes are released Lowered blood pressure Normal respiratory rate Normal body temperature Body working easily and aging slowly
All these changes are designed to prepare your body to freeze, fight or run. But many of these changes occur in response to non-threatening lower stressors, too.	*All these responses maintain long-term health, conserve energy, and bring balance to your body's systems.*

My work focusses on teaching practices that help people sustain balance in their lives, so they feel composed, confident, capable, and inspired. It's my way of helping people unlock more of their potential and enjoy a successful and happy life. When you know how to proactively alleviate the effects of everyday stress and turmoil, it puts you firmly back in the driver's seat rather than being at the mercy of whatever life throws at you. And that's the most powerful confidence boost you can give yourself.

The model I use to help people understand what a balanced sense of well-being is involves exploring intellectual, emotional, physical, and spiritual health, and determining whether you are on what I call an upward spiral of potential or a downward spiral of despair. Once you can identify if you're on a downward spiral, you can quickly and effectively turn yourself around and get back on an upward spiral. Throughout my career, I've been fortunate to experience and learn how important this delicate mind-body balance is for health and well-being. And I've learned many practices that help ensure this sense of holistic well-being can be maintained.

So, as you can see in the context of maintaining the physical aspect of well-being, I'm not simply talking about fitness, but being in touch with the messages your physical body sends you. Although physical exercise is a starting point for many people and a gateway to holistic health, it's also a way to become more embodied and mindful. I know this because it's the path I took.

Taking part in sport was an enormous part of my life when I was growing up. When I didn't receive any awards for being studious, I would always be recognised for my contribution to the athletics team. Where I couldn't compete academically, I could win a gold medal in the swimming pool. I didn't care too much about being the height of fashion; my favourite shoes were my turquoise and yellow Nike runners. Brightly coloured running shoes are a dime a dozen now but in the '70s they were very special!

I remember getting a pair of running spikes for my birthday. I could not have been happier. They were white with a red stripe down the side and were light as a feather. I loved the smell of the leather and just wearing them seemed to make me run faster. Happiness to me was running around the race track or donning my tie-dye speedo swimsuit and doing lap after lap in the pool.

But my journey into teaching health and well-being began in London in the '80s as an aerobics instructor. I was working in an advertising agency and the best part of my day was half-past five in the evening when I would jump on my bike and duck and weave through the traffic from Oxford Circus to Covent Garden to attend classes at Pineapple Dance Studio. The studios were in a former pineapple warehouse, hence the name, and the open spacious warehouse interior housed lots of different rooms with whitewashed brick walls, mirrors, wooden floors, and beautiful arched windows. For those in the know, the dance centre was simply known as Pineapple. It was modern and trendy and as soon as I walked in, I was transported to another world. These people didn't wear corporate clothes and sit behind desks, they were vibrant, healthy, creative, and hip. There were fit bodies and brightly coloured lycra everywhere, and yes, we did wear leg warmers and headbands! Teacher's voices could be heard shouting instructions above loud music in the various studios, and the whole place hummed with energy. Most evenings after work I would peddle to Pineapple and enter the vibrant throng of men and women ready to move and dance to loud music.

I didn't dislike working in advertising, it was also a fun and energetic environment to be in, but my heart was calling me to prepare myself for other things. I wanted to be one of those instructors. Once I'd done my teacher training, I signed up to teach aerobics classes after work hours wherever I could. Looking back, I can see how it was a natural part of my make-up to feel strong, capable, and exhilarated through physical exercise. It helped me cultivate a strong energetic presence that has been a major asset in my ability to stay on an upward spiral of potential. I loved long-distance running and swimming at school, so solitary moments of oneness and connectedness with body and mind, and being in a meditative zone was also something I experienced through sport.

In my early twenties, I began dabbling in yoga, but I was often the youngest person in the class, and it was something my Mum did, so I wasn't convinced it was for me. I was curious though because it offered something I was familiar with from my hours of swimming and running. I didn't understand at the time how the mindful state of yoga was so familiar and inspiring to me, and it was only later that I realised why. I had spent hours in my high-school years swimming up and down a fifty-metre pool, listening to the sound of my breath, focused on the repetitive rhythm of my stroke, and the feeling of the water. Unbeknown to me I had learned to be alone with my thoughts and to keep bringing my focus back to my breath in a moving meditation up and down the pool.

Years later, teaching meditation is an enormous part of my work and mindfulness is a household word. But as a teenager, I only knew it as a zone I went into, where the whole world seemed to disappear and all I was aware of was my body and my breath. You don't have to don a pair of running spikes, swim laps, or join a dance class to foster this sense of union between body and mind, although don't let me stop you. As you'll soon discover, your body and breath are your best friends when it comes to being mindful and soothing your nervous system.

It boils down to this. Are you happy that your body is working hard, suffering damage, and aging quickly because you live with worry, stress, or a victim mentality? Or would you like to develop the capacity to take control of your thoughts, move easily through challenging emotions, and regenerate your body? The choice is yours. If you're experiencing terrible trauma or depression it would be wise to seek help. However, when it comes to our day-to-day self-doubt, stress, worry, and frustration the first step is to remember that these are experiences shared by everyone, not wrong, simply misguided. To move through these challenges we need to *PAY ATTENTION* to our thoughts, *EMBRACE* our emotions, and *EXPLORE* our feelings. When we take this inner journey we see that we always have a choice about how we think, feel, and act, even in difficult times.

Chapter 16
Step 3: Connect

Airing out the Spiritual Aspect

By 1989 I was married to my husband, he was in the army and I was running my fitness enterprise. It was the start of a journey that would lead me through all aspects of understanding what well-being means.

Wherever we were in the world I could set up my exercise classes and personal training sessions and I had a captive audience of army wives. Soon we moved from England to Hong Kong, where my husband was serving with the Gurkha Engineers. The Gurkhas are soldiers from Nepal who for the last two hundred years have been recruited into the British army. They are known to be fearless in combat, but I experienced the other trait they are famous for, their good nature and kindness. Their white teeth would always shine from behind a big smile, delicious spicy aromas would waft from their homes, and our squadron gatherings were always made more enjoyable by their love of games and family fun. I'll never forget playing in a football match with their wives, all in their beautiful saris!

Aerobics classes were all the rage, and I was regularly teaching classes of up to fifty people. And then came an unusual request. I was asked by the commanding officer of my husband's squadron whether I would teach a class for the soldiers. Of course, my Nepalese was non-existent, and English was the soldier's second language, but hey, that wouldn't be a problem, all they needed to do was stay in time with the music and follow me. Fearless in battle they might be but following aerobic dance moves did not come easily to them. Rather than being in the gym with a sound system, microphone, and a sea of women in lycra before me, I found myself outside on the drill square, faced with a squadron of soldiers in their gym shorts. But I knew this was going to be fun and I also knew they'd give it a red-hot go.

The instructions to follow me they took quite literally, so I quickly realised that scratching my head or making any movement that was not part of the dance routine needed to be eliminated. We all had a great time that morning, dancing in the sunshine, and there were cheers of delight when they finally managed to link all the moves together into a short routine.

But it wasn't their dance moves that impressed me. These brave warriors had a softness and inner peace about them that radiated wherever they went. My husband had the good fortune to travel to Nepal and spent months hiking to mountain villages to help install irrigation systems, so the villagers could have running water. He came home stunned by these gracious people who treated him like a treasured guest. Their lives were hard in the harsh environment of the Nepalese mountains, and yet they were the happiest most generous people he'd ever met.

As well as being exposed to the Nepalese culture, Hong Kong at that time was a hot, humid melting pot of eastern and western influence, creating a cross-cultural way of living that was exciting and new to me. I loved nothing more than to roam the streets of Kowloon or Hong Kong island. One minute I'd be surrounded by ultra-modern buildings and the next I was down some narrow alleyway, encased on either side with tiny little shops crammed from floor to ceiling with rolls of fabric, kitchen utensils, or fake watches. The smell of food combined with the heat and the hustle-bustle of this city was intoxicating.

Hong Kong is where you'll find the teachings of Buddhism whose followers use meditation to purify the mind, overcome suffering, and gain a deeper understanding of the nature of life. Lao Tzu was a Chinese philosopher recognised for founding the philosophical system of Taoism. This tradition, followed by many in Hong Kong, advocates living a simple life and understanding the nature of humans, and our place in the universe. This unique island steeped in history is full of temples, some are ornate and magnificent while others are small and unassuming. I was fascinated by the many spiritual traditions that have been practiced for generations by the people living on this tiny piece of land. My exposure to these different cultures and ways of life began to open my mind to the fact that we humans are searching for something elusive, but very necessary, to our happiness. And I began to understand that it wasn't going to be gained by having more money, getting a promotion, or buying a new car.

When I talk about the spiritual aspect of us, I'm not referring to religion, although for some this avenue will provide great meaning. I've talked about understanding and finding balance in the intellectual, emotional, and physical parts of ourselves, and mentioned how these aspects are intricately entwined, meaning they never work in isolation. It's my experience that when these first three aspects are in balance a natural transition occurs and we find that it is possible, and far more enjoyable, to live beyond the confines of the ego.

What do I mean by ego? In the previous chapters, we've talked about the conversations that go on in your head, generated mostly by the rich biography of your life, and that these conversations dictate the way you think, feel, and act. This is how our ego comes out to play. When you see someone honking their car horn and shouting out of the window because they've been cut off in traffic, that's ego at play. In their mind, they've been diminished or wronged and need to build themselves back up. Why? Because something happened to that person in the past that made them feel belittled, and they decided that they never wanted to feel that way again. Now as an adult this person's identity is that of someone who aggressively shows their authority.

When you notice that your friend has stopped calling you because she's got a promotion and is mixing in different circles, that's ego at play. In her mind, she feels more worthy and successful, so she needs to eliminate anything that could endanger her new persona. When someone puts you down or criticises your success, that's ego at play. This person can't feel happy for you because they don't feel happy about their life, so they make themselves feel better by bringing you down.

The ego creates identities for us to cope with such things as pain, confusion, disconnection, and loss of love. It is assembled by all the beliefs we have about ourselves; it is the identity that the mind has constructed, but this identity is false because we are more than just our minds.

Whenever you are angry and feel the need to hit back, it's because you've bought into a belief that the mind has constructed, and you feel the need to regain a sense of security. Which is, of course, a false sense of security. Your mind may tell you that you're not appreciated by your partner, which leads to feeling offended and resentful. So, to bring yourself back to an even playing field and feel more secure, you insult him or her. Equally, whenever you feel inadequate, fearful, unworthy, stupid, or any demeaning, self-critical emotion, it's because you're believing the stories your mind is telling you, and the ego has come out to play. When we believe these thoughts with even the slightest conviction, it serves to boost the ego. In these situations, you might buy into a false sense of security by sabotaging your success through procrastination, laziness, and making yourself small, or you'll diminish yourself and limit your sense of purpose and potential.

We can see people's egos playing out everywhere in society. Especially in our political system. At the 2016 Democratic National Convention, Michelle Obama first said her now-famous catchphrase, "When they go low, we go high." She was referring to the tactics of politicians trying to undermine her husband, Barack Obama. The divisiveness and spitefulness that these politicians were demonstrating came from ego and was a clear example of ego being fear.

Whenever you mindlessly listen to the habitual negative chatter in your head about your inadequacies and failures the ego will always have you going low, manipulating and manoeuvring your way through life to quell your fear and feel better. What's important is to recognise when your ego is at play, and you'll be able to do that now because you're going to be *paying attention* to your thoughts. You're going to *embrace* your emotions and *explore* your feelings. This will free you up, giving you the capacity to live beyond the confines of the ego, where you will naturally *connect* more deeply to yourself and others.

Understanding this and being able to identify when your ego is at play will improve your life and unlock your potential. Your ego is going to become your best friend because you'll know when you're out of balance, and you'll use any egoic thoughts, emotions, and feelings as signposts that will direct you back to balance. This process will have you stare your ego directly in the eye and choose to come back to your true nature of a kind, loving, caring connection with yourself and others. This is the spiritual aspect of yourself and I'm inviting you to *connect* with this part of yourself because it's the only place you'll find a genuine sense of security. It's the only place you'll find deep forgiveness of yourself and others, and it's the only place of genuine connection with yourself, your fellow humans, and the universe. This place of calm, composed, presence is your true nature, spirit, source, or whatever you prefer to call it, and it's the foundation of your potential.

I remember being in a hotel in Kowloon one weekend, I was twenty-six and heavily pregnant with our first child. Although I was extremely excited about the prospect of having a child, I wasn't enjoying being pregnant, especially in the heat and humidity of Hong Kong. It was early morning and I looked out the window of the hotel. As is often the case in Hong Kong, I felt I could almost reach out and touch the person in the next building. There was a series of interweaving freeways around the hotel already full of traffic, and from my vantage point I could look down onto a mass of tiny houses and shacks below, their makeshift roofs of corrugated iron, wood, and tarpaulin like a patchwork quilt beneath me. As always, in this city that never sleeps, activity was everywhere, and people were rushing around pushing overloaded carts and weaving in and out of traffic on bikes, despite the already soaring heat. Water was thrown into the alleyways and steam rose from the many stoves cooking up a storm. Even though I was above this scene in another building, I could imagine the sweet, spicy, earthy smell of the laneways I'd come to know so well. And then I noticed on the tiniest piece of grass right under the freeway a lone man immersed in a tai chi sequence. He was an old man and wore baggy grey trousers and a vest, his face was open, his skin smooth, and he had an aliveness about him that belied his age. As he drew his arms through the air and moved his body, he did it with effortless grace and ease. But what struck me was that this man was in a state of focused harmony and bliss, as if the hustle and bustle around him didn't exist.

It's been moments like this in my life that have compelled me to understand the deeper complexities of the mind and explore the meaning of happiness and success. There I was in the cool comfort of a hotel, eagerly awaiting one of the most exciting times of my life. All was well in my world, and yet this man in his vest and trousers, who presumably lived in one of the tiny shacks I could see, surrounded by noise and hard work, seemed infinitely happier and more content than I. He appeared to have a handle on life that I hadn't yet grasped and embodied calm, peace, and control. From my window, I could see he had a faint smile on his face as if he were amused at the absurdity of life's problems and was able to find happiness within himself, despite the interference and chaos around him. I watched him for a long time, captivated by his energy and presence.

By the time I returned to England and later came to live in Australia I was a firm advocate of the ancient arts of tai chi and qigong. I had done my yoga teacher training and explored many meditation techniques and was slowly understanding the answers to the questions about life I'd been pondering. I was drawn to the look on that man's face as he did his tai chi under the freeway because it portrayed the same blissful feeling I had as a child on that hillside in the Lake District. He was in a meditative state, at one with the flowing movements of his body, in tune with his breath, and absorbed in what he was doing. His mind was undistracted by the frenetic activity of a world waking up around him; he was in touch with his spiritual essence.

Children can do this easily because they'll happily become engrossed in 'being' in the moment. They might be petting their dog or pressing their hands in the sand, staring at the sky, or singing to themselves. Unfortunately, in a world driven by action, adults will often snap their children out of this state, believing they're daydreaming, not concentrating, or wasting time.

Memories of our life experiences begin to take up space in our once untainted minds and living in the present moment becomes more difficult and is something that needs to be practiced. That's what the man doing tai chi under the freeway was demonstrating. He was engrossed in his morning ritual of training his mind and body to come back to this very natural, but often forgotten, state of pure awareness, from where he could gain free access to spirit and potential.

When I teach meditation classes I often tell my students that we are learning meditation not so we can sit for hours and hours in a blissful state of relaxation and peace, although that is of course a nice by-product; but the real reason we learn to meditate or reach meditative states through practices such as tai chi, is so that we can engage in the big wide world feeling clear, composed, open, kind, and loving. Being in a classroom and learning to meditate, whether your classroom's a group, an online course, an app, or a moment of tai chi on a patch of grass, serves to remind your mind and body what balance, control, and composure feel like in a safe and easy environment. So, when you venture out into the world and life challenges you, the skills you've learned through your meditation practice are second nature to you, and you can respond to life with clarity, confidence and composure.

The process of practicing meditation is a little like going to the gym, but you're developing your brain and mind-body connection rather than your biceps. Most people go to the gym to maintain a strong and healthy body. The gym is their classroom, then they can go out into the world and enjoy a better lifestyle. Meditation is the classroom in which you train your mind.

The neuroplastic nature of the brain means that we can improve and strengthen it in ways we never thought possible. Research is showing that mindfulness-based stress reduction and meditation help increase the size of the hippocampus, the part of the brain involved with memory storage and retrieval. When functioning well, this part of the brain is thought to create an appropriate context for memories. This then helps us to form a reasoned storyline of what is and is not dangerous. In people suffering from depression, studies have shown that this function suffers because the hippocampus shrinks, a little like a broken limb will shrink in a cast. It is also thought that meditation facilitates a decrease in brain cell volume in the part of the brain called the amygdala, which is responsible for detecting fear and storing emotions and memories linked to sadness and anger. Research shows what I have experienced, and my clients have reported, that stress levels reduce, and psychological well-being is enhanced through meditation.

All this indicates that meditation not only changes the brain but positively changes our perceptions and feelings as well. Furthermore, studies have revealed that the part of the brain linked to kindness and compassion lights up like a Christmas tree when we meditate. This is just the tip of the iceberg, the ongoing research about the adaptability of the brain is mind-blowing, pardon the pun. What's exciting is that this research is showing that our potential is not set at birth, because we have the power to strengthen and improve our brains. Combined with all the physical benefits we've already discussed, such as lower blood pressure, strengthened immunity, reduction of stress toxins, and feeling happier, this means our lives are greatly enhanced and our potential increased by the simple practice of meditation. Think about that for a moment. As well as all the physical benefits of meditation, how would your life improve if you experienced less fear and self-doubt and instead were able to enjoy inner peace, resilience, and confidence? How would your relationships, mothering, career, or business benefit from these simple changes? Even this small amount of research is enough to encourage us to take ourselves to the "brain gym" regularly and learn to meditate. So, let's get started with a simple practice.

Later I'm going to show you a meditation that will enable you to access your spiritual nature more deeply. But to begin with I'm going to show you a practical and easy way to help your mind become focused and calm. To do this we need to give it something to concentrate on, and the breath is the obvious thing. It's always available, it's portable, and it's free!

A simple meditation practice.

Read the instructions below and then try this for yourself. Be open to the fact that your mind is going to chat away and this may not be the blissful experience you're expecting. That's okay we're just getting started, and with practice, your meditation time will become more and more enjoyable and fruitful.

For easy listening, if you would like to download a free audio recording of this meditation (and all the meditations in this book) go to: www.rutholiver.com.au/recordings or scan the QR code at the back of the book.

Exercise 5 – Simple Meditation

1) Make sure you won't be disturbed for at least five minutes. Sit or lie down, making sure your body is aligned, supported, and comfortable. Let your mind roam around for a couple of minutes, not trying to stop any information coming to you, just letting sensory information come and go as it pleases.

   Spend a few moments sighing and as you breathe out focus on letting your body relax and surrender to the surface that supports you.
2) Now, instead of being engaged with your wandering mind, tune into your breath.

   Where does your attention land when you do that? It will be unique to you. Your attention may go to your chest, your rib cage, or your belly. You may feel your breath predominantly in the back or sides of your body or sense the feeling of filling and emptying. There's no right or wrong way to do this, you simply need a focal point. Find your focal point and let your attention rest there.

3) Tune into the sensation of your breath moving in and out of your body as if you were observing it down a telescope and nothing else existed. It's important not to try and change your breath and make it deeper than it wants to be, just breathe normally. This will help you with the first step of awareness that we've discussed throughout this book. Your job is to *pay attention* and notice when your mind is distracted.
4) Let your body fill gently like a balloon filling with air, then emptying as you watch your exhale fall easily from your body. If you feel the urge to sigh, go ahead and do that.
5) Notice when your mind has been taken away from its focus on your breath and has been hooked by a thought, a sound, a feeling in your body, or any other distraction. When you realise this has happened, as it will regularly, simply bring your attention back to your breath focal point. Continue focusing on your breath with curiosity, noticing when the mind is distracted, and using those distractions as signposts back to your breath. Become more curious and interested in your breath than you are about the things that distract you.
6) Finish your meditation by sending a big sigh through your whole body.

A good time to do this Simple Meditation is when you wake up. When you practice this for a few minutes each morning it enables you to lay down some foundations for your day that put you in control of your mind. This will help you manage the challenges your day may bring with more ease and control.

A few years ago, I had the pleasure of helping conduct a meditation session in a men's prison in England. I met several of the inmates but one of them had a profound effect on me that I'll never forget. His upbringing had conditioned him strongly, and because of the very violent nature of his life, he had created an identity for himself of someone who was incredibly tough and intimidating. His reputation went before him and the other men in the group told me he was feared greatly by the inmates. Eventually, he found his way to a meditation teacher in the prison, and it was through this teacher that I was invited to participate in their weekly session. The prisoner told me how violence and intimidation had been the go-to tools that made him feel he was someone who mattered. It was hard to imagine this person he described because what I saw before me was a kind, considerate, composed, and emotionally intelligent man. All the men spoke about their lives trapped in the identity of being a criminal, some of them serving multiple sentences before they were able to break free of their conditioning, in large part through meditation. These men had benefited from the physiological changes that take place in the brain during meditation, affording them more emotional regulation and a greater ability to form a reasoned storyline of what is and isn't dangerous. And importantly, they gained access to innate qualities of compassion and kindness, putting them back in touch with their spiritual nature.

This experience made me reflect on the way we detach from our spiritual nature and fellow human beings. Of course, there are some people who for their safety, and ours, need to be removed from society, but there are many who have simply had exceedingly difficult lives and are emotionally scarred by their experiences. Their scars form a protective identity to which they relate because it's the only way they know how to feel safe. You and I also have scars. I have scars that during my life have had me comparing myself unfavourably to others, feeling incapable, self-conscious, and inadequate. Yours may mean you avoid speaking in public or don't like to push yourself beyond your comfort zone, perhaps you doubt yourself or believe your life is just the way it is, and you can't change it. Those who end up in prison have often had more traumatic experiences during their lives; they have bigger scars and have created identities that get them into more trouble. I felt sad as I left the prison that our answer to this problem is to lock people up behind high walls and barbed wire.

We are all carrying pain. It's part of our collective experience. The man I met in prison explained to me how meditation made him see that he wasn't that intimidating, bulked-up, violent person. Through meditation, he was able to peel away the layers of belief and emotion, just like the layers of the onion, that had him locked in misery. Even though he's going to be in prison for a great deal of his life, confined behind bars, he's rekindled his spiritual nature, unlocked his potential, and is an inspiration to those around him. Against all odds, he's re-training his mind, developing his brain, and giving himself the gift of coming home to his spiritual nature of forgiveness, love, hope, and inspiration.

Paul Collins is a former Royal Marine and founder of the organisation Thrive Inside. He continues to do important work unlocking the potential of people in the criminal justice system. (If you feel moved to support this valuable work, go to Paul's website for details: www.thriveinside.org)

When we talk about the spiritual aspect of a person it will mean something different to everyone. Some will find it difficult to describe and others will know exactly what it means to them. It's certainly not my intention to tell you what it is or to impose my view of it onto you, but rather to guide you through a process that will enable you to arrive at your own experience. The process I will guide you through will enable you to see that identifying with your unhelpful thoughts will only serve to pull you further away from this deeper level of consciousness and peace.

As you practice meditation, the process of becoming more intimately acquainted with the intellectual, emotional, physical, and spiritual aspects of you will enable the disruptive mind to drop away. As you *PAY ATTENTION*, *EMBRACE*, and *EXPLORE* you'll peel away the layers of conditioning and *CONNECT* to a place that's free of fear and resistance. Here you'll experience coming home to your true nature of timeless, limitless presence, full of love and hope. In this state, your path to potential is a wide-open sunny stroll.

Just like my friend in prison, this is a stroll you can take at any time, and I sincerely hope you do, because what you have to offer the world is important. After all, it's your very own unique potential. The butterflies won't stop, but they won't appear as often, and you'll be able to soothe them at will and carry on your way.

A word of encouragement before you begin

Before you picked up this book you already knew there was something greater to be had than a life bound by your lack of confidence, feelings of inadequacy, self-doubt, or any myriad of unhelpful emotions. We are never plagued by these things when we're born, they are conditions of our own making. The blueprint of your true nature resides within you. Control, composure, love, happiness, connection, all those things you know to be your spiritual aspect are available to you. This miraculous design that exists within you never goes anywhere. No matter what has gone on in your past, or is going on around you right now, you always have the necessary tools to come back to your true nature, and from there respond calmly to life.

Often you don't have language for what resides inside of you, wanted or unwanted. It doesn't matter, you know that living on autopilot will never fulfill you, and when you nurture your well-being and tune into your inner wisdom, the comfort and empowerment you'll find there will serve you far better than trying to gain outer control.

The inner journey that's required for you to remember your true nature is passive, quiet, still and reflective, so you may still doubt it. Your conditioned response in the action-orientated world in which you live will keep telling you to "do something!" I urge you to be kind to yourself. Trust that by being still and coming home to your true nature daily, by doing dedicated practices, and by bringing active practice into your life, you *are* doing something. Something far more powerful and fruitful than any amount of outer manipulation will ever achieve.

What you are seeking in yourself won't ever be fulfilled, because this is a never-ending journey of self-discovery. But don't be disheartened because when you put the simple practices in this book into action you will enjoy more freedom and happiness. With a little practice, patience, and persistence, when you least expect it, you'll wake up to the singing of the birds feeling refreshed and alive, instead of in the dead of night feeling alone and anxious. Soon, in the not-too-distant future, you'll realise you've stopped yelling at the kids and that you no longer get anxious about your workload. At some point, you'll take comfort from knowing your worry is a shared human experience that can be soothed quite easily, and you'll notice that your usual self-doubt and uncertainty have been overshadowed by composed confidence.

Keep on exploring. Trust this inner path to your potential, because even though you'll never reach the end, the gifts you'll receive along the way will fill you up.

Enjoy the journey!

APPENDICES

Appendix 1
Doing the Inner Work

Small daily changes make a big difference and in this section of the book, I'm going to walk you through some practical exercises that you can easily integrate into your daily life to "air out" the intellectual, emotional, physical, and spiritual aspects of you. It's one thing to understand why this is important and take on board the prolific amount of research that tells you how valuable it is to manage your mind, but it's quite another to put processes in place that will enable this to happen.

Most women struggle with the concept of giving back to themselves. If on top of your job you're also caring for elderly relatives or you're a mother, it's even harder to find time for yourself! But having a quick, simple spiritual practice, such as meditation, that enables you to fill your reservoir, is the most important element in unlocking your potential and thriving in life. I know how many roles and responsibilities women take on and how dedicated you are to caring for the people you love. That's not going to change, and nor should it, it's who you are. That's why I focus on making these well-being practices as simple, effective, and as manageable as possible; so you can easily move your well-being up your list of priorities without feeling guilty or neglecting those you care about. After all, if I told you that you'd have to go to bed by sunset, ready for your first practice at sunrise, you'd probably have some serious reservations about starting!

Do you remember I talked about how practicing meditation was no different from going to the gym? Only you're developing your brain and mind-body connection, not your biceps. Well, in this part of the book I'm going to show you the exercises you need to do each day at the mind-body gym. I've called this "Dedicated Practice" because you need to dedicate some specific time to these practices. Try to think of these new practices that you're going to incorporate into your daily routine in the same way you'd think of cleaning your teeth, or getting dressed in the morning, so they become second nature to you. In conjunction with these, I'll show you how you can implement practices into your everyday life that will enhance your Dedicated Practice. I've called this "Active Practice" because they are small, but significant changes that take no extra time as you carry on with your daily routine.

With persistence, you'll be more alert to the wisdom and messages these practices bring as you go about your activities and interactions. Once you integrate these new habits they'll become second nature, and you'll be amazed at how you'll begin to control your thinking, manage your emotions, and feel more embodied and inspired. As this occurs, you'll naturally come home to your true nature, the part of you that knows exactly what makes your heart sing and your spirit soar. And then you'll be on the open road to your potential. However, none of this will happen if you don't take action!

You are about to begin an inward journey of exploration into thoughts, emotions, feelings, and your unique and personal spiritual realm. Before we begin, I want to reiterate that this is a journey of discovery. There's no quick fix that will take away all your worries and self-doubt overnight. But what I can tell you is that this inward journey will deliver. You will not be disappointed as you begin to take control of a mind that can be reckless and emotions that run wild. This journey will positively enhance your life in ways you didn't know were possible.

Before you begin with these practices, I encourage you to do this short, written exercise so you have a clear idea of what it means to be intellectually, emotionally, physically, and spiritually healthy rather than unhealthy. Not only will this help you identify the negative states to which you might have become numb, but it will also help you set your compass on a new course because you will be able to see what's possible for you.

Exercise 6 – The Four Aspects Health Check

With a pen and some paper, sit somewhere quiet where you won't be disturbed. Draw a quadrangle on your paper big enough so that you can write in each square. Along the top of the top left-hand square write Intellectual, along the top of the top right-hand square, write Emotional, along the bottom of the left-hand square write Physical, and along the bottom of the right-hand square write Spiritual. Now draw a diamond shape within the quadrangle, cutting each quadrant into a triangle. In all the outer triangles put a minus sign and in the inner triangles put a plus sign. So, you'll end up with a shape that looks like this.

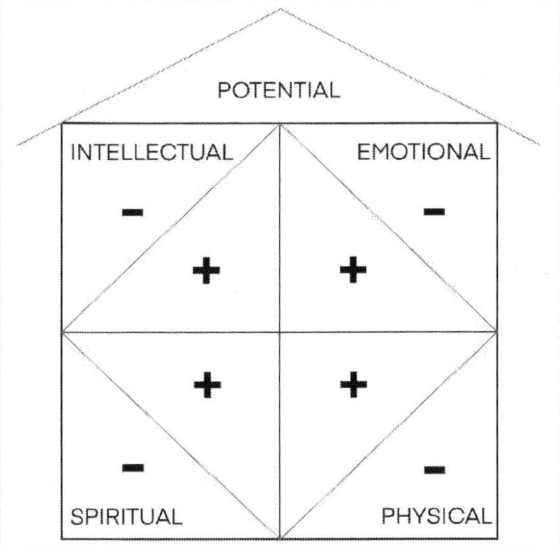

Figure 2: The Four Aspects of Well-Being – *showing where to map your healthy and unhealthy states that can occur within these four aspects.*

Begin to think about the different aspects of yourself and fill in the triangles with all the words that describe how you feel when you are in a healthy or unhealthy state in each of these aspects. The minus sign depicts an unhealthy state and the plus sign a healthy state.

Begin with the intellectual box and think of words that describe how you feel when you are experiencing being intellectually unhealthy. All these words are going to go in the outer triangle of the Intellectual square, where you've put your minus sign. There's no right or wrong with this exercise, when I do this in my courses there's an enormous range of words that end up on this diagram. For example, feeling unhealthy intellectually can cause some people to feel muddled, ignorant, unintelligent, confused, even competitive, or angry. Health in this aspect may be described as capable, clear, sharp, clever, productive, or even powerful.

Work your way around the quadrangle filling in each aspect, first with the unhealthy qualities in the outer triangles, then with the healthy qualities in the inner triangles. Remember that the spiritual aspect is very personal to you. Fill this triangle in last, as the other aspects will often feed this one. When you've finished, you'll have a diamond shape full of all the words that represent feeling whole and healthy. Draw a circle or bull's eye in the centre of the diamond and then a spiral that moves up to the top of the page. Living within this inner diamond is what keeps you on an upward spiral of well-being and enables you to reach for more of your potential every day.

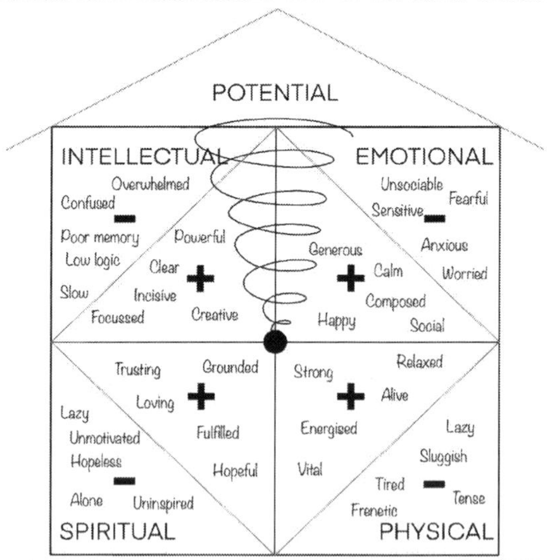

Figure 3: The Four Aspects of Well-Being – *showing how health in these four aspects can lead to an upward spiral of well-being and potential.*

Do you remember at the start of the book I told you about a quote that said we need to visit each aspect of ourselves daily if only to air it out? Filling in this diagram gives you a very real sense of what happens for you when you fail to do the inner work required to air out the four aspects of being human. It's also an exciting insight into what's possible with a little determination. So, let's visit these aspects more intimately and begin doing the inner work that will set you on an upward spiral of well-being and potential. Let's put it all into practice!

Appendix 2

The Intellectual Aspect – Overcoming Monotonous Conversation and Mind Chatter

Things are changing, thankfully, but for too long one of the most tragic things about our primary education systems is that nowhere on the curriculum did children get the opportunity to learn they have control over their thoughts and mindset. This concept was something I learned through some painful experiences. Maybe you're still having those painful experiences, if so, I'm glad you've stuck with me this far.

During the time I was working in advertising in London I remember agonising for weeks over asking my boss for a pay rise. I would imagine myself in his office and rehearse in my mind what I wanted to say. I knew I was due a pay rise, I was good at my job and there was no reason why I shouldn't have one. And yet for weeks, I would go over and over this conversation in my head. One day I'd feel bold and brave, the next dejected and full of self-doubt, then I'd be angry and sick of myself for being so pathetic. I felt distracted at work and resentful of the people who I knew were earning more money than me. I'd swing like a pendulum from telling myself that it didn't matter, I should be happy I had a job, to feeling frustrated and unappreciated.

Unbeknown to me at the time, all these feelings and emotions that made it so difficult for me to ask for more money, were unconsciously generated by the memories from my life experience. Stored away in my unconscious mind were stories that told me I didn't deserve a raise. I'd sit on the underground on my way to work giving myself a pep talk and preparing my pitch, only to whimp out the moment I walked into the office.

Eventually, I plucked up the courage to knock on my boss's door. Breathing hard, tongue-tied, and uncomfortable, I made my request. I was given a raise, no questions asked! All the endless conversations in my head, the worry, self-doubt, and fear, had been generated by my own inner beliefs of inadequacy and unworthiness that had nothing to do with the outcome of a pay rise.

Perhaps you've had a similar experience. Don't get me wrong, just because you're going to learn how to manage your mind doesn't mean you won't ever feel helpless and hopeless at times, I still do. But had I known then what I know now, I would have done things very differently. I would have stopped trying to boost my confidence with pep talks and rehearsals and instead done the much more effective inner work that I'm going to show you now. I would have realised that I needed to *pay attention* to the chatter in my mind and that having butterflies in my stomach didn't mean there was something wrong with me! Instead of beating myself up about them, and pushing through the resistance, I would have stopped and tuned into my inner world. I would have paid attention to my thoughts and written out a Thought Cascade (chapter 14), enabling me to identify the depth of the criticism I was aiming at myself. I would have tried to *embrace* my emotions with compassion and curiosity and *explore* the physical sensations they were causing in my body (chapter 15). And, I would have spent my time on the train doing some of the practices

I'm going to teach you here, which would have enabled me to understand the truth of the situation rather than the one I was making up in my head. My mind would have been clear, my nervous system soothed, and my resistance dropped. All of which would have put me back in control of the situation, boosting my confidence, and making the whole experience more enjoyable. Had I done this inner work I would have been able to confidently knock on my boss's door and eloquently ask for my raise. Instead of suffering through weeks of angst, I could have had my pay rise in the bank!

Earlier in the book, I talked about there being two types of thought or conversation we have in our heads. Let's revisit them now so I can show you how to bring them under control, so rather than them being reckless and unhelpful, you can learn to be more aware of them, which immediately gives you a greater sense of control. As you immerse yourself in these practices a new type of thought will come to you. I call it "Inspired Thought."

Monotonous Conversation

Imagine your thoughts are like a gentle stream, a never-ending and continuous flow of memories, reflections, and beliefs. On the surface of the water, there are patches of bubbling turbulence as the stream navigates its way around rocks and pebbles, just as we navigate our way around daily life, relationships, work, and family. Monotonous conversations are a little like this turbulent surface water. They're the negative conversations you have with yourself as challenges arise on a day-to-day basis, and with a little practice, they are easy to catch. I used to have these conversations more when our boys were young. I'd be cleaning the house, whilst the rest of the family were seemingly doing far more enjoyable things, and these conversations would develop into a tirade in my head that told me, "no one else cleans the house!" "In fact, everyone just leaves their mess for me to clean up!" Of course, these thoughts also have their roots in the unconscious mind. The trigger was the cleaning, the thought was "I'm not appreciated," the emotion was anger, and the physical reaction was muscle tension and no doubt raised blood pressure! All this, not because of the mess around the house, but because of a story generated by my unconscious mind about being unappreciated. But with a little practice, we can catch these thoughts as they bubble up and choose a different way down the stream.

One of the amazing things about your mind-body system is that it's very quick to learn, and when you use that to your advantage, positive change can be rapid. When you give your mind-body system some clear instruction and practice repeating that instruction, it will quickly adapt.

Vince Lombardi famous American football coach and general manager of the Green Bay Packers led the team to three NFL championships and Super Bowl victories in 1967 and 1968. He became a national symbol of single-minded determination to win. He said "practice does not make perfect. Only perfect practice makes perfect." Not that you need to feel the pressure of perfection here, but you see what he's getting at. If you continually repeat something, it becomes ingrained. This is why it's important to be aware of your internal dialogue because if it's continually negative, these patterns will be repeated and become a habit. If you can identify and practice managing your key monotonous conversations, those you regularly have, you'll notice that all internal conversations become more manageable.

So, this is where we begin to *pay attention.* As you now know, the mind and the body are intricately interconnected, and it's often through the discomfort of your unwanted emotions that you can identify a monotonous conversation. As I think back to the time I would begrudgingly clean the house feeling angry and unappreciated, I can sense even now how those thoughts and feelings would have made my blood pressure rise and my body tense up. Tragically, we do this to ourselves frequently, so I'm going to help you identify when you might be sabotaging your mind and body in this way. I'm going to talk about exploring emotions more a little later, but for now, you're going to use their discomfort to alert you to an unhelpful monotonous conversation.

You will never be able to stop thinking and that is not the point of these mindful practices. You will, however, be able to regulate the relentless barrage of thoughts that invade your mind, unchecked and uninvited, by becoming more conscious of them. It is only by being more conscious of the workings of your mind that you will be able to gain control of it. Not only are you *not* trying to stop your thoughts you are going to learn to actively *pay attention* to them.

Dedicated Practice - The Conscious Inventory

- **Use this to help calm Monotonous Conversation**

Sharpening your conscious attention is the key to managing your mind, your emotions, and enhancing how you engage with life. Being present, aware, or mindful are all words used to describe this state of consciousness. Because your magnificent mind can ruminate and project and make up some negative stories, becoming more conscious of the sensory information that comes to you moment-by-moment is an important skill to refine.

This simple exercise will help put the brakes on any unhelpful wandering of your mind and enable you to live with your attention focused more clearly on the present moment. Why is this useful? Because when you live in the present moment you are in control of your experience and will be able to live with more ease, peace, and enjoyment in your life.

All you need to do this exercise is a pen and paper. It can be done at any time anywhere and as long as you are not engaged in conversation it doesn't matter what's going on around you. If you need a break from your work or want some time away from your computer screen, it's a very relaxing and productive way to take a break. The wandering mind affects the emotions and the physical body, but this exercise is relaxing and rejuvenating because it tames any reckless thoughts that impact your emotions and physicality.

Exercise 7 – The Conscious Inventory

Sit down with your pen and paper and simply begin to *pay attention* to everything you are noticing. As your thoughts, feelings, or observations become apparent, write them down. This is simply a process of recording everything you are aware of as it comes to your conscious attention.

For example, my inventory right now as I sit at my computer would be - left hand, shoulders, glasses, heavy legs, hungry, cold fingers, kettle boiling, mouth, urgency, Paris. As you can see it's just a list, some of my observations are thoughts and feelings from within and some from what I notice around me. I'm not going into any detail about why these things come to my attention, I'm simply writing them down. Paris came to my attention because there's a coaster on my desk that I got while I was in Paris. But the story of the coaster is not important, I'm not going to let my mind wander back to my time in Paris and start writing about what a wonderful experience I had, or where I might like to go on my next trip because that would take me out of the present moment.

Try not to go looking for things to write down, simply notice what stimulates your senses, moment-by-moment. Keep your gaze soft and let your observations emerge on their own. By doing this exercise you are simply training your mind to be more conscious of random thoughts that often go unnoticed and hone your ability to live in the present moment. Give it a try now and make it a regular practice in your life.

Do this practice every day for one month and then weekly. It will take you anywhere from sixty seconds to five minutes.

Mind Chatter

Back to the analogy of the stream. Just beneath the bubbling surface of any stream is a body of water that cannot easily be seen but is nonetheless just as turbulent. This water is full of debris that it's picked up as it moved downstream. It carries with it the history of its journey: silt, weeds, plant life, twigs, and even rubbish. The volume of debris in the deeper water will determine whether the stream moves easily on its journey or whether it's impeded by carrying so much litter with it. Our unconscious mind is like this deeper body of water, in that it is holding our life experience, much of which can impede our journey downstream. The way we know that we aren't moving freely downstream is when we become aware that we are experiencing emotions such as fear, anger, anxiety, guilt, or shame.

While emotions can be strong, the thoughts behind them can be confusing, unclear, and difficult to pinpoint. Thoughts emerge uninvited from the unconscious mind in reaction to an event, such as when I wanted to ask for a pay rise. As a young twenty-year-old needing to step out of her comfort zone, I could feel my frustration, but I had no idea that my doubts and fears came from the deep, unhelpful mind chatter that was playing over and over in my head.

Dedicated Practice - Stream of Consciousness Writing

- **Use this to reveal unconscious Mind Chatter**

We made a start at identifying mind chatter earlier in the book during the Thought Cascade exercise. If you haven't done that exercise, go back to chapter 14 and familiarise yourself with it now. Next, we are going to explore the deeper realms of the unconscious mind more fluidly and spontaneously, by engaging in Stream of Consciousness Writing.

Unlike the Conscious Inventory, where the aim is to be extremely focused on listing one thing at a time as it comes into your awareness, this time you're going to let your mind run free. This process is one of self-compassion, allowing our unconscious mind to be heard in this way is like listening to your friend's deepest insights, without interruption or judgment. Exploring the deeper layers of your unconscious mind in this way is liberating and assists you to make sense of things, helping you access your innate sense of understanding, intuition, and trust.

Sometimes when I do this exercise I may write about the same subject for a long time, answering questions and making sense of things. At other times my emotions want to be heard and getting my feelings onto the page is very healing. Often an idea will come to me and I'll flesh it out and get creative. On another day my writing may not make much sense at all, or my to-do list will end up on the page. Every day is different, but every time I do this exercise, I benefit in surprising ways. From the very practical such as formulating ideas for my work, to the more obscure, such as understanding myself and my life. Doing this form of writing never disappoints. I always feel clearer and calmer, and any resistance I may have been feeling is diminished after doing this exercise. And one of the most beneficial powers stream of consciousness writing gives you is the ability to engage in more helpful internal dialogue. When we bring unconscious thoughts and feelings into consciousness and give them space to be heard, the mind enjoys more order, and habitual uncontrolled thought patterns and destructive mind chatter release their hold over us.

You have unconscious conversations with yourself all day, every day, and you're getting a sense of the exhausting journey they can take you on. You are now aware of how these unconscious stories can colour how you feel about yourself, and often create unnecessary stress to your physical body. By engaging in this exercise, you'll bring what is in your unconscious into consciousness, and thereby begin to observe your thought processes rather than be unwittingly embroiled in them. You'll begin to discern how you want to think, feel, and act rather than simply leaving it to the whim of your uncontrolled mind.

Read these instructions and then try this exercise yourself.

Exercise 8 – Stream of Consciousness Writing

Find a quiet place where you won't be disturbed and have your pen and paper ready. First, close your eyes and take three deep breaths. When you open your eyes begin to write. As your pen comes to the paper let everything that comes to mind out onto the page. Simply write whatever comes into your head. Unlike the Conscious Inventory, where you were listing your sensory observations in a more orderly way, this time let your thoughts and feelings emerge from within and run free. Allow your writing to be uncensored and free-flowing. As you do this, you'll notice the vast reach of your mind or the speed at which it can move from one thought process to another. Don't worry if your thoughts don't make sense or seem to have no relevance in your life, it can be astonishing what comes out and onto the paper when we permit ourselves to do this. There's no need to fuss over neat handwriting or punctuation; in fact, it's better to just let your pen flow across the page continually, bringing to light whatever you're thinking or feeling.

If you find this challenging or your words are not flowing don't worry, this in itself is a starting point, and you could write about not knowing what to say…

Or try asking yourself a question for some inspiration. Here are some examples to get you started:

- What matters most in my life?
- What role does my mind play in my life?
- What am a grateful for?
- When did I last step out of my comfort zone?
- What would I do with my life if I felt confident and didn't care what others thought of me?
- If I could advise my teenage self, I would say…
- How important is my physical body?
- What am I most concerned about at the moment?
- I'm glad I'm me and appreciate myself because …
- In a perfect world, I would feel …

The key is not to over-analyse the process or censor your thoughts. Permit yourself to write, unchecked and uninhibited, and go with the flow. You can set yourself a certain amount of time for your writing or keep going for as long as you wish. You'll find you don't have to think about when to stop, it will happen quite naturally.

Do this practice weekly or whenever you feel like it. Write for as long as you wish.

Appendix 3

The Emotional and Physical Aspect – Living comfortably with Emotions and Feelings

For many years I struggled to gain benefit from meditation because I was under the impression that I had to somehow stop the relentless stream of information that came to me when I closed my eyes. Later I understood that this information would only diminish if it were first given space and recognition. This is something you'll observe from the writing practices. If when you've finished writing you close your eyes for a while, you'll notice it's a little more peaceful in there than usual. Let me put it another way.

A few years ago, we were the fortunate custodians of a foster dog called Molly who had spent much of her life being neglected, fending for herself, and moving from one dog shelter to the next. She's a Labrador, Staffordshire Terrier cross, with jet black fur and soft brown eyes, and we fell in love with her the moment she arrived at our home. For many weeks Molly would do a rigorous check of the house every time she returned from an outing. She would roam around, going into each room, sniffing into the corners, and checking under furniture. Once she'd satisfied herself that all was well, she would settle in her bed and have a nap.

In my workshops and courses, people often tell me how they've tried to meditate but their mind is so busy it's impossible to focus, let alone relax. Often, as I was, they have been trying to suppress or ignore their thoughts in order to find some peace. You may have heard phrases such as "let your thoughts go," or "allow your thoughts to drift by." This can be hard to achieve, especially if you have a lot going on in your life. So, I want you to try the exact opposite! As you begin your meditation, do what Molly did every time she came home and allow all your senses to be on full alert. Molly knew she couldn't relax until she'd addressed her memories and feelings, and her way of doing that was to sweep the house. You are going to sweep your mind, not because you want to sweep it out, but so you can *embrace* what's there. Instead of thinking of your thoughts and emotions as your enemy, and noises, images, and feelings as something to get rid of, *embrace* them, just like Molly.

When a friend or loved one feels emotional, we innately know that mostly they just want someone to support them and be present with them. They are not looking to have their problem solved but to have some company while they feel their emotions. Children understand this well and will often be drawn to simply sit with someone or hold a person's hand when they sense there is something wrong. When you *embrace* your emotions and *explore* the often-ignored feelings they produce in your body, without any attempt to judge, control, or change them, you are in effect embracing yourself, just as you are. In this way, the monotonous activity of your mind will begin to dissipate, and your nervous system will be soothed. You will also be able to hear the messages your wise voice of reason, creativity, and control has for you.

The process of allowing your thoughts into your experience as a pathway to clarity and peace is not a new phenomenon. The Yogis have known this for centuries and Rumi, the 13th-century Sufi Mystic and poet described it in his famous poem *The Guest House.* As you practice your meditation see if his words resonate with you.

The Guest House

This being human is a guest house.
Every morning a new arrival.
A joy, a depression, a meanness,
some momentary awareness comes
As an unexpected visitor.
Welcome and entertain them all!
Even if they're a crowd of sorrows,
who violently sweep your house
empty of its furniture,
still treat each guest honorably.
He may be clearing you out
for some new delight.
The dark thought, the shame, the malice,
meet them at the door laughing and invite them in.
Be grateful for whoever comes,
because each has been sent
as a guide from beyond.
-Jalaluddin Rumi (translation by Coleman Barks - The Essential Rumi)

Dedicated Practice - Breath, Body Meditation

- **Use this to be more comfortable with any Emotions and Feelings**

The very act of settling to meditate often sets up the expectation that it's going to be a silent and peaceful experience. However, when you sit still, close your eyes, and become quiet, you may notice that it's not as peaceful as you imagined! At this point let go of any attempt to remove the sensory information you experience. Instead, lay out the welcome mat and *embrace* it. Your breath and your body are valuable tools when it comes to taming an uncontrolled mind. Negative emotion is rooted in fear and most fear comes from allowing the mind to rake over the past or venture into an unappealing future. Using the body and breath as a focal point enables you to practice paying attention to the moment your mind has become distracted. Instead of letting your thoughts run riot, you are now honing the skill of living in the present.

When you realise you're distracted, embrace it. Whether it be a noise, a sensation, a memory, or an emotion, use the distraction as a gentle reminder to bring your focus back to your meditation technique, in this case, your breath, and your body. Think of your mind like a muscle. This is a process of training the muscle of consciousness through choosing where you want your attention to be.

During this Breath, Body Meditation your senses will still engage with other information; that won't stop just because you're now concentrating on your breath and body. But you now have some control over your mind because you'll be paying attention, so you'll be responsive when your mind is distracted and bring your attention back to your breath and body. This continual interplay between where you are trying to keep your attention and where your roaming mind wants to go is not a battle between the conscious and the unconscious mind. Treat it more as an exercise of observing where your mind is moment-by-moment. Are you conscious and focussed on your breath and body or unconsciously letting your mind drift? Simply notice which is at play and choose where you want to place your attention. Give it a try now and make it a regular practice in your life.

For easy listening, if you would like to download a free audio recording of this meditation (and all the meditations in this book) go to: www.rutholiver.com.au/recordings or scan the QR code at the back of the book.

Listening to a guided meditation in this way can be extremely helpful because your mind will be more easily occupied by the instructions and less likely to roam.

Alternatively, you could ask a friend or family member to read the instructions to you, making sure there's plenty of quiet space between each instruction, giving you time to explore.

Exercise 9 – Breath, Body Meditation

Find somewhere as quiet as possible to sit or lie down. If you're sitting, make sure your body is supported and your spine is upright. Settle into your chosen position making sure you're comfortable and your body feels balanced, so try not to slump in a chair. Close your eyes.

Allow your senses to pick up on all the information that comes to you. Perhaps images, tastes, smells, feelings in your body, noises, and of course arbitrary thoughts. Let the very natural process of your mind exploring occur and notice the information that comes to you without any judgment or an agenda to get rid of it. (*Long pause here.*)

Take your attention out into the wider world and notice what you experience. (*Pause*). Next, bring your attention to the country you are in and simply notice what arises. (*Pause*). Now let your attention absorb the region you live in *(pause)* and then your city or town. *(Pause).* Then the street you are in, (*pause*), the building you're in, (*pause*), and the room you're in, (*pause*). Now feel the surface or the chair beneath you, (*pause*). Then notice your own body (pause), and finally bring your attention fully to your breath.

Let your attention be on your breath. (*Pause*). At no point are you trying to force your breath to be fuller, just breathe normally with your belly gently expanding on your inhale and softening with your exhale. Notice the beginning of your inhale and follow it without effort to the top. As you breathe out, let your breath fall easily from your body. (*Pause*).

Now, tune into your physical body, simply noticing the sensation of your own body. Initially your mouth, jaw, and behind your closed eyes. As you breathe out, let your attention rest on the whole of your face. *(Long pause*). And then the whole of your head. *(Pause).* Start to move your attention down through your body, each time you exhale taking your focus to the next obvious place. *(Pause).*

Notice the neck and shoulders. *(Pause).* Breathe out and let your attention move down your arms, to your hands and fingers. *(Pause).* Your inhale is full but easy. Breathe out and notice your torso. *(Pause).* Then your hips. *(Long pause).* As your breath leaves your body, move your attention down your legs. *(Pause).* Notice your feet and your toes. *(Pause).*

Your attention may be drawn to specific parts of your body, perhaps because they are holding tension or pain. If so, place your attention on that part of your body as you breathe out, remember you are embracing everything you experience. (*Pause*).

After a while, go back to the focus on your breath as you inhale and your whole body as you exhale. (*Pause*).

If you find yourself distracted by a thought or something that's worrying you, that's ok, it means you're *paying attention* and you've noticed that your mind is wandering. Any time your attention is hooked by thoughts, feelings, or emotions, *embrace* them, not trying to force them away, and gently move your attention back to your breath. *(Pause).* Watch your inhale and be with your whole body as you exhale. *(Pause).*

Slow your exhale down, letting it fall very softly from your body as it soothes your nervous system. Allow your body to surrender to the surface that's supporting you.

If your worry or concern is causing a physical sensation in your body such as a churning stomach or a knot in your chest, simply notice the feelings, not trying to stop or suppress them. *Explore* them with a sense of curiosity. *(Pause).* When you're ready, move your attention back to focus on your breath as you inhale and your whole body as you exhale.

Stay here as long as you wish, simply noticing when your mind has been distracted, acknowledging those distractions, and training your attention back to your breath and your body. *(Pause).* Gradually, you'll notice that your body will naturally relax and any frenetic activity in the mind will be quieter and unwelcome feelings in the body will begin to dissipate.

Enjoy exploring this more and more.

Challenge yourself to do this practice for ten minutes every day for one month, so it becomes a positive habit in your life.

Do a longer practice each week beginning with the Conscious Inventory or the Stream of Consciousness Writing; once you've finished, without interruption begin your Breath, Body Meditation.

When doing this breath and body meditation it's important not to strive for a calm, relaxing experience because that will only create an energy of resistance. Remember that the natural process of your mind becoming calmer, your nervous system soothing, and your body relaxing happens through the process of embracing all sensory information, then gently reminding yourself of your breath and body focus, rather than willing yourself to relax.

Active Practice – Breath, Body Meditation as you go about your day

- **Use this to practice living with more ease and peace in your daily life**

Just as you would go to the gym to improve the strength of your legs, replacing unchecked thoughts with conscious, clear, intentional thought is like going to the gym to increase the functionality of your brain and improve the capacity of your mind.

Many years ago, when I was a personal trainer, my focus was always on what is called functional training. Rather than just training people to have great-looking arms or lose weight, which is a great side effect, I was always more interested in improving their quality of life by helping them be strong, agile, and flexible. Functional exercise trains your muscles to work together and prepares them for daily activities by simulating regular movements that happen in daily life. Squatting, balancing, reaching, and lifting all become easier when functional fitness is integrated into a workout routine. It's one of the reasons I went on to become a Pilates instructor, because the core strength, poise, and posture you learn in any Pilates studio are directly relevant to your enjoyment of life. So, when I became a meditation teacher it was only natural to me to help my clients take these mindful practices into daily life in a functional way.

As I mentioned before, the mind is quick to learn, given the right instructions you will naturally take what you learn and apply it in your life. But it's also especially useful to practice actively in daily life. When you become more conscious by concentrating on a task at hand, moment by moment, you train your mind to stay present, and not wander off in unhelpful or distracting directions.

You may not have much time to devote to your well-being. Although I can assure you, if you make even a short meditation a daily habit, you'll notice such a difference in your life you won't need me to persuade you to stick with it. But you don't have to be sitting in a quiet room with your eyes closed to engage with these practices; wherever you are, whatever you're doing, every single moment offers you the chance to live with more conscious attention. In fact, engaging in these practices while out and about doing your daily activities adds another layer of understanding for your mind and body, because you are receiving different sensory information each time.

When I sit to meditate at home and begin by noticing what I can hear or feel, the experiences are repetitive. The same tightness is there between my shoulder blades, the same dog is barking over the fence, the noises in my home are familiar. But when I'm on a train or a tram or sitting in a waiting room, each time is different and offers me the opportunity to hone these skills even more. There are so many opportunities in your daily life to practice being more conscious, there's no reason to believe you don't have the time to learn how to manage your mind and allow yourself to live with more ease and peace. And it's always my aim to make that process as simple and effective as possible for women like you, with full lives.

Here are some ways in which you can integrate functional meditative practices while going about your daily activities. As you incorporate this new way of being in your life, be alert to how this more meaningful level of engagement with your daily activities uncovers a deeper level of clarity, wisdom, and acceptance within you. You might even find yourself enjoying everyday tasks that are usually mundane.

Exercise 10 – Breath, Body Meditation as you go about your day

- Any time you're travelling you can engage in a breath, body meditation. Instead of sitting on the train or tram, aimlessly scrolling through your phone, do the conscious inventory exercise in your head. Simply begin to label each sensory experience as you notice it. You might want to close your eyes, but it's not necessary. Then follow that by bringing your attention to your breath and your body and do a few minutes of meditation.
- Instead of sitting in traffic getting agitated, bring your focus to your breath and your body. **Please do not close your eyes in this situation! Keep your eyes open.** Be very conscious of all sensory information as you drive, your hands on the steering wheel, your feet on the pedals, your back in the seat, the detail of what you see, and the feeling of your breath in your body.
- Any time you find yourself in a waiting room, instead of reading the out-of-date magazines on the waiting room table, practice being mindful. This is especially useful if you're nervous about your appointment. In the dentist's chair, waiting in the queue in the supermarket, sitting in the car park as you wait for your kids to finish their sports practice, or when you're walking. Every moment of the day offers you the opportunity to check your uncontrolled thoughts and build the muscle of your mind. And you'll arrive at your destination with a clear head and a calm demeanour.

Active Practice – Daily Activities to Hone the Mind

- **Use this to Sharpen your Mind and live more Consciously**

Use the everyday activities you engage in as opportunities to practice being more conscious. As you clean your teeth, wash your hands, or do the dishes, how attentive can you be to the task at hand?

I challenge you to clean your teeth, have a shower, do the washing up, clean the car, vacuum the house, weed the garden, or undertake any household or personal activity without chatting in your head about something unrelated to the task at hand. Because these activities are second nature to you, in other words, you no longer need to consciously think about how to do them, they are now on autopilot. This means the mind is free to roam untamed and unchecked as you engage in these tasks. As we've discovered it's the untamed and unchecked mind that causes our worry and anxiety. So, chores that we usually do on autopilot are a great place to practice taming the mind.

Exercise 11 – Daily Activities to Hone the Mind

Whether you're doing the ironing, walking the dog, brushing your teeth, doing the dishes, cleaning your car, mopping the floor, showering, or gardening, your brain doesn't have to think too hard about how to do these everyday activities. This leaves time and space for your mind to start thinking of other things. So, instead of letting your mind run amok, bring your attention back to the task at hand, whatever it is, and use it as a time to breathe and focus.

For example, when ironing that same pair of trousers you've ironed many times before, this time be very conscious of the feel and weight of the iron in your hands, the warmth, smell, and the texture of the cloth, and the material becoming smooth. As you do the washing-up focus all your attention on the feeling of the water and the dishes. When you're having a conversation with someone, practice listening intently to what they are saying, giving the person the gift of your full presence. As you clean your teeth concentrate fully on the task at hand.

Every day is an opportunity to engage with the present moment by being more focused on your daily activities. When you live this way, you deepen your mind-body connection, alleviating the uncontrolled wanderings of your mind that can cause anxiety. This allows you to engage with life in a more relaxed and poised manner.

Balancing the Scales

As discussed earlier, all emotions manifest as a sensation in the body and often these manifestations are our first indication that something is disturbed. Perhaps you wake up with a churning stomach because you have a job interview, or you notice you feel slightly sick at the thought of having to make a presentation at work. Maybe you feel rage churning inside from a comment made by your friend that you can't forget, or you have a deep knot in your chest from an argument you had with your partner. Sometimes these emotions and their accompanying sensations are just there, and you're not sure why. Of course, you want to get rid of these unpleasant feelings so you might ignore them or try and pep yourself up, just like I did day after day when I was trying to ask for a pay raise.

Having now practiced the Breath, Body Meditation you will be more comfortable embracing the myriad thoughts, feelings, and sensations that continually arise moment-by-moment in your mind and body. You may notice that this internal approach is yielding some pleasant results, enabling you to feel more in control of your thoughts and at ease with your emotions. This exploration provides a gateway to the subtle messages that can arise from sensations in the body. So, let's keep going.

Bring to your mind something that is bothering you now, and then imagine there's an old-fashioned balance scale in front of you. In the left-hand dish of the scale imagine that you are placing all your worries, troubles emotions, and the physical manifestation of this thing that is bothering you. Maybe anger, frustration, and the headache it's giving you. Whatever it is, place it all in the scale, and in your mind's eye watch as it tips with the weight of your troubles. Now imagine placing as many contrasting thoughts, feelings, and sensations in the right-hand dish. Maybe a sense of freedom, joy, calm, and relief, and you get a sense of how the scale can come back to balance.

We live in a world of contrast, everything has an opposite. The night is the opposite of day. Summer is the opposite of winter. We cannot know happiness without knowing sadness. We cannot know confidence without feeling self-doubt, just as we cannot feel love without knowing the contrast of fear. We are conditioned to be attached to what we would deem as more positive experiences and reject any negative experiences we have, and we work hard to manage ourselves and our lives to ensure this happens. However, when we believe the scale must be tipped to the positive side for us to cope and be happy, living in fear of what will happen if it gets weighted down on the negative side, we create an enormous amount of resistance within ourselves. This resistance contributes to feelings of anxiety and stress, placing strain on the physical body that will block our enjoyment of life. Learning to be with all our experiences, thoughts, emotions, and feelings without labelling them as good or bad, wanted or unwanted, right or wrong is the key. In this way, we train ourselves to be at peace with whatever arises in our lives.

When we can sit in meditation and *embrace* our emotions and *explore* the sensations they produce in the body, in the spirit of everything being equal, without attachment or rejection, we find genuine control and harmony. This is not a false control of holding, manipulating, and forcing the scale the way we want it to go, but an inner control that enables us to feel safe with everything. Practicing in this way cultivates our capacity to feel comfortable with all of life's experiences, however challenging. It enhances our ability to respond creatively rather than reacting from a place of resistance. Of course, situations will arise that are difficult, and we will continue to be challenged and suffer from time to time. But when we engage in life with this more balanced mindset there's no longer the same level of fear or rejection around the difficulties that arise, and we can live a fuller life.

We spend most of our lives looking outside of ourselves or trying to change our external circumstances to bring back the balance of our scale. It takes some practice for the more natural, internal process of genuine balance and harmony to emerge. Be patient with yourself and enter this meditation with curiosity, rather than an agenda to learn a new skill. You may fall asleep, which is fine. Gradually you'll broaden your capacity to experience a full range of emotions and feelings, and importantly you'll be able to enjoy the benefits of internal balance in your everyday life.

Dedicated Practice – Balance the Scales Meditation

- **Use this to help your mind and body dissipate difficult emotions and feelings**

This next meditation is based on yoga nidra, an ancient practice originating in India, sometimes referred to today as yogic sleep. The roots of yoga nidra can be traced back to Sankhya philosophy first written down around 700 BC. Now a mainstay practice for most yoga teachers it's a process during which the body becomes very relaxed, negative emotions are released and the nervous system is soothed.

This next meditation has elements of yoga nidra in it and will also enable your body to become very relaxed. Another aspect of yoga nidra is to locate contrasting feelings and sensations in the body as you meditate. During the meditation, you'll be doing this too. Investigating opposite feelings and sensations such as lethargy as opposed to vitality, tension as opposed to relaxation, or chaos as opposed to calm.

When the mind and body can *embrace* and *explore* in this relaxed state there is a deep understanding that occurs that helps us recall this way of being when out in the big wide world. What this equates to is being able to stand in the face of troubles that would ordinarily upset you and remain calm and relaxed. Being conscious of the enormous range of internal emotions and feelings available to you, despite what goes on around you, enables you to be with the challenges that come across your path with more ease and acceptance. Practicing in this way gives your mind and body a more balanced view.

You don't need to have a full-blown encounter with these different states. Please don't worry if you are not fully experiencing what I'm asking you to engage with. Remember that a large percentage of our daily thoughts have a negative quality to them, leading to unhelpful emotions and uncomfortable physical sensations. Now you are going to practice opening your mind and body to a wider variety of experiences than you otherwise might have.

As you explore your unique emotions and feelings and their opposites, simply go with what's there. One day you may find you've got a sore neck, can you find the opposite of the soreness? Or you may feel anxious in the pit of your stomach, can you find the opposite of that? Perhaps you'll feel frustrated, see if you can be open to a contrasting experience? This meditation will reveal to you the range of emotions, feelings, and sensations available, that ordinarily you may not be aware of. This enables unhelpful feelings and emotions to settle or dissipate more easily, and with practice, the same will happen in your daily life, so you can live more comfortably.

If you wish you can download an audio recording of this meditation, and all the meditations in this book by scanning the QR code at the back of the book or by going to: www.rutholiver.com.au/recordings

Or you could make a recording of your own. If you do, make sure there's plenty of time to take in each instruction followed by lots of silent space. It's in the silence that the understanding happens. Once you've listened to your recording a few times, so you understand the directions, try it on your own.

Exercise 12 – Balance the Scales Meditation

Find somewhere as quiet as possible to sit or lie down where you're unlikely to be disturbed. And if it's not quiet or you are disturbed, that's okay, it will only add to the richness of your meditation by giving you something else to *embrace* and *explore.* If you're sitting, make sure your body is supported and your spine is upright. Settle into your chosen position, making sure you'll be comfortable, and then close your eyes.

Allow your senses to pick up on all the information that comes to you, noises, images, tastes, feelings, thoughts, and emotions, without any judgment or an agenda to get rid of these experiences. *(Pause.)*

Bring your attention to your body, particularly the weight of your body and the balance of your body. Notice the surface on which you are sitting or lying, notice which parts of your body are touching a surface and which parts aren't. *(Pause.)* As you breathe out take your attention down into your body and spend a while exploring the feeling of your whole body. Let your breath guide you to explore more deeply into the feelings and sensations in your body. *(Pause.)*

Now you're going to work your way very slowly through your body, spending time exploring different areas of your body. You might like to spend four or five breaths exploring each area.

Begin with your face, spend some time simply exploring your face taking time to explore sensation in your mouth, back into your jaw, and behind your closed eyes. *(Pause.)* Notice your forehead and then sense the whole of your face. *(Pause).* And now notice the whole of your head. *(Long pause).* Next, move your attention down to your neck *(pause),* shoulders, *(silence),* arms, and hands. *(Pause.)* Take your attention to the front of your torso, *(silence),* the back of your torso, *(silence),* your hips, *(silence),* legs, *(silence),* and feet. Be aware of your breath, let your breath gently fall from your body as you turn your attention inward. *(Pause).*

As you do this, you'll notice that your body naturally becomes more and more relaxed, especially as you exhale. *(Pause.)* Simply allow your long, slow exhale to relax your body and e*mbrace* and e*xplore* this feeling of deep relaxation that you're experiencing. (*Pause.*) How does it feel to be relaxed in this way? Try not to analyse or think about it too much, simply experience being very relaxed. (*Pause.)*

And now, let's begin to explore contrasting feelings in your body. *(Pause)*

Bring into your mind and body the feeling of being alert and alive. You may feel very subtle movement in your body as you do this. What do you experience when you bring a feeling of liveliness into your body? (*Long Pause.)*

Let these different feelings unfold to whatever extent you can. *(Pause).*

Now can you allow both of those feelings to be present? Deeply relaxed and at the same time vital and energised. Let your whole mind and body engage in this experience. *(Pause.)* The scales are balanced, you're not attached to one feeling or the other, both are there and you're simply observing yourself having this capacity for relaxation and energy at the same time. (*Pause*). Quietly notice these experiences that are available to you. *(Pause).*

Turn back now to the state of rest in your body and spend a few moments with your breath. (*Pause*).

Next, take your attention to thoughts and feelings of confidence. Bring into your body the energy and feeling of being confident. Perhaps remember a time or place when you previously felt this way. Or is there someone in your life who helps you feel more self-assured and resilient? Or can you just imagine what it would feel like to have a more confident outlook? (*Pause*).

Now allow your attention to turn to thoughts and feelings of lack of confidence. Maybe you remember a time when you felt this way, bring those feelings into your body now? What does it feel like to have little confidence? (*Pause*).

And now, allow both of those experiences to be present, confidence and lack of confidence. Both at the same time, not attached to one or resisting the other. Become the observer of these states rather than being fully engaged in them. Bring the scales back to balance and let your mind be the spectator of these experiences. Have a sense that you are no longer the person who is having these experiences but you're now watching them. (*Pause*).

What do you experience in your body when you tell yourself – life is easy? *(Pause).*

What emotions, feelings, and energy do you encounter when you consider that life is easy? *(Pause).* Let this experience unfold to whatever extent you can. *(Long pause).*

And now bring to mind the concept of life being difficult. What do you experience when you consider this. *(Pause).* Notice how your body feels when you tell yourself life is difficult. *(Pause)*

And again, can you be aware of both? Life is difficult, life is easy. Simply noticing that both those thoughts and all the emotions and feelings that come with them, are available to you. *(Long pause).*

Spend some time being with all these experiences, embracing everything just as it is. *(Pause.)* Observe yourself having thoughts, emotions, and feelings. Use your gentle breath and long slow exhale to go inward to a still, quiet place where you can watch these experiences moment by moment, rather than being embroiled in them. (*Long Pause*).

Reflect on the journey you've just taken and note what your mind and body now understand more clearly. Are you getting a sense of your true nature as peaceful and composed? Despite all experiences, this calm, accepting state is always there waiting for you to arrive. (Long *pause*).

Still feeling relaxed and breathing easily, imagine feeling this way in your everyday life in both challenging and pleasant moments. (*Long pause*.) You may wish to recall a certain situation that often has you hooked by unhelpful emotions and feelings. Imagine yourself in that situation connecting to this sense of peaceful composure and balance at that time. (*Paus*e).

And now bring your focus back to your breath and then back to the feeling of your body on the surface you're on and the room around you. Gently open your eyes, stretch, move and come back to your day.

Do you remember - The 4 Aspects Health Check exercise back in chapter 8? If you haven't done it, I encourage you to go back and do it now, because applying what you find in the health check to this meditation can be very valuable.

Why is this important? Well, as we've discovered, many of our thoughts have a negative quality to them. So, if you're seeking financial freedom but the unconscious inner conversation you regularly have with yourself says something like – "you're dreaming, how on earth are you going to make more money in your position!" You're hardly going to feel motivated or notice opportunities that might afford you financial freedom.

Or let's say you want to lose weight, get fit, and have more energy but your unconscious inner voice berates you, saying – "dream on, you've been saying that for years and haven't changed a thing." You get a sense of how demoralising and demotivating these unconscious words can be, and why this voice is referred to as the inner critic.

Unfortunately, when we let our reckless mind control us in this way, these unconscious words that play over and again in our head, inform our actions. Our actions soon become our habits and we wonder why we're not able to be more successful.

Gandhi said -
"Your beliefs become your thoughts,
Your thoughts become your words,
Your words become your actions,
Your actions become your habits,
Your habits become your values,
Your values become your destiny."

If we want our habits and standards and ultimately our future to be other than what we are currently experiencing, we must start with our thoughts and train ourselves to bring balance to the mind.

Once you've practiced the Balance the Scales Meditation a few times, bring into the meditation the aspects of your life where you would like to see change. For example, if it's financial freedom you're seeking, use your senses to paint a very clear picture in your mind's eye of what financial freedom looks like. Where are you, how are you living now you're financially abundant. How does it feel to have lots of money, to never have to worry about money? Bring the feeling of abundance into your experience.

Now, think about the lack of money in your life and notice how that makes you feel. What do you experience when you think of this lack?

Spend a few moments going back and forth in your mind between the experience of lack and financial freedom.

Now, bring your focus to your breath, let your mind and body relax, and spend some time simply observing that a vast array of thoughts and feelings are available to you. Become the witness of your unhelpful thoughts alongside your more empowering thoughts. In this way, we learn to become more discerning about what thoughts we engage with.

When you relax and allow yourself to become acquainted with the negative picture that you've bought into, and alongside that paint a picture in your mind's eye of what you desire, you can have a more honest and empowering conversation with yourself. Now your actions will be congruent with this more balanced view of what's possible, habits and values will change, and you feel more inspired and motivated.

I use this process often in my meditation. If I'm feeling nervous, I remind myself what confidence feels like, and come back to balance. If I'm feeling resentful, I remind myself what contentment feels like, and come back to balance. If I'm feeling upset, I remind myself what peace feels like, and I find balance. It's a wonderful way to train your mind and body to find balance in all aspects of life and know that underneath the negative thoughts we habitually have there are positive, helpful thoughts that lead to inspired action and greater success in life.

Dedicated and Active Practice – Mountain Pose

- **Use this to bring focus and energy into your daily life**

Mountain pose is a simple, foundational yoga posture. So, don't worry I'm not going to ask you to stand on your head! And if you've never done yoga that's fine, too. All this posture requires is that you stand. Or you can incorporate many of the elements of this posture while sitting if you prefer. The reason I'm using the mountain pose as something that you could practice in daily life is that there are many opportunities during your daily activities to bring the elements of this posture into your body and mind. After all, that's what yoga is all about, experiencing the union of the mind and body and assimilating what you learn on your mat into your everyday life. For example, while I'm sitting here typing this page, I've just bought some of the elements of mountain pose into my body and immediately I feel more embodied, focused, and comfortable.

Follow the instructions below and you'll see that standing in your own body can provide a lot of feedback and is a great container in which to become more conscious, grounded, and balanced in mind and body.

Once you become adept at assimilating the postural points of this pose into your body, I encourage you to bring them into your life as much as possible. Bringing your attention back to your body in this way not only focuses your mind but also enhances energy that can become depleted when the mind is scattered. If you're about to enter an interview, the energy of this posture will help you feel composed and even powerful. If you're tired and slumped at your desk the elements of this pose will lift and energise you. When feeling frenetic and overwhelmed the elements of this pose will ground and calm you. Not to mention that your body will love the postural alignment that occurs. As well as noting the physical points of this posture, notice how it feels to stand in this way, and enjoy this balanced posture and supported feeling in your body whenever possible.

Exercise 13 – Mountain Pose

If you can, do this exercise in bare feet and stand on an even surface. If you are unable to stand you can remain seated with your feet on the floor.

Place your feet hip-width apart, so that your heels are aligned with your sit bones in your bottom. We're going to work from the feet up, aligning the body. Slightly lift your toes and spread them wide as if you had webbed feet so you can feel the four corners of each foot, the two back corners of your heels, the ball joint of the small toe, and the ball joint of the big toe. Place your toes very lightly back down on the floor. Work to bring even weight through these four points on each foot, notice whether your weight is in the front of your feet or the back, and see if you can distribute your weight evenly through these four corners of your feet. Let your feet enjoy the balanced and even contact they now have with the floor and imagine you have roots from the bottom of your feet holding you firmly to the ground. This attention to your feet alone will enable your whole body to begin to organise itself into a more balanced and aligned state.

Now have a sense of a line of energy that comes from the arch of your foot, up the inside of your legs, then up your spine to the crown of your head. So, the crown of your head becomes the top of the mountain. Check to see whether your shoulders are rounded forward, closing your chest and heart, or maybe they are forced back like a soldier. Circle your shoulders a few times and let your shoulders drop gently down and find a slight lift in your heart as you do that.

Take note of your lower back and check you're not sticking your bottom out too much or feeling tightness in the lower back. Let your tail bone feel heavy, and as you do that softly draw in the navel. You're not squeezing your buttock muscles or pulling your tummy in hard. Simply let your tail bone drop a little and become aware that you have tummy muscles, engaging them slightly. There's no tension in your knees or any part of your body. You're standing tall and aligned but without rigidity in your body or tension in your muscles.

Continue to be conscious of the points of alignment you've set up and settle into the comfort of feeling balanced, stable, and upright. As you breathe in, have a sense you are rooted to the ground through all four corners of your feet at the base of your mountain, your lower body feeling grounded and solid. As you breathe out, sense a feeling of energy up the insides of your legs. Aware of your active core, open heart, and soft shoulders. Focus on your spine lifting with your crown being the top of the mountain. Fully conscious of your body and breath. Stay here for a few minutes with your eyes either open or closed. If you feel a little wobbly with your eyes closed, keep them open, looking at something at eye level with a very soft gaze.

Stand or sit in this solid, stable, and yet relaxed and open state for a few minutes. And remember this posture and feeling in your body so mountain pose can become Active Practice any time you find yourself standing still in your daily life.

Pick and choose from these practices which ones you would like to do on any given day. Five minutes of Conscious Writing followed by a ten-minute Breath, Body Meditation will set you up well for your day. If you are feeling a sense of worry or upset, doing the Balance the Scales meditation to explore the feelings and sensations of your worry, and upset and finding their opposites will help. Standing in Mountain Pose for a few minutes after your meditation will help you become more grounded in the present moment and is a nice conscious transition into the activity of your day.

Active Practice – Finding the Zone

- **Use this to unlock your potential in daily life**

Earlier in the book, I described to you a state that athletes call "being in the zone," and if you're a sportswoman you may have experienced this "zone" yourself. It's another way of describing a meditative state in which all resistance falls away. When you are in the zone the mind is clear and calm, the body is energised but also very relaxed, and movement is effortless because perfect balance and harmony have been found.

One of the ways I experience this zone is when I'm doing hill riding on my bike. It's quite easy when riding up a steep hill on my bike with my lungs pushed to the limit, and my thighs screaming to become overwhelmed by these feelings. But when I practice *paying attention* to the negative focus of my mind and choose to *embrace* the feelings in my body and then *explore* for opposite feelings, I can find this zone.

At the same time as my breath feels laboured, I can also feel the expansion in my lungs as I inhale. At the same time as I feel the muscles of my thighs burning, I can also feel the power in my legs. At the same time as I feel the effort in my body, I can also feel ease and effortlessness. In the Balance the Scale Meditation I asked you to spend some time observing and being with all the experiences you had during the meditation? Wanted and unwanted, being with everything as it is. This is no different, it's just that now you're using this skill in a very practical way in life.

Exercise 14 – Finding the Zone

Wherever you are, whatever you're doing, rather than trying to gain control by resisting or pushing externally, allow yourself to abide in a still, quiet place of observation where you'll enjoy all the magnificence of your true nature. You'll enjoy clarity, ease, composure, energy, and a release of your potential, not from force but with effortless joy. Whether your passion is riding hills on your bike, walking, painting, skiing, surfing, sewing, swimming, playing golf, or gardening, any activity is an opportunity to find the zone and enjoy your true nature.

Being in the zone is vastly different from zoning out! If I were riding my bike on a bike path in Melbourne while daydreaming about riding in the Swiss Alps, that would be zoning out. Being in the zone is a state of deep focus and concentration, where nothing else seems to exist other than your body and your breath in a moving meditation.

As you paint, play golf, do gardening, walk, ride your bike, swim, kayak, run or lift weights, whatever your activity of choice is, choose periods when you actively focus. Cast your mind back to Mountain Pose and become aware of your feet on the ground, the alignment of your body as you walk. Be conscious of the length of your spine, your relaxed shoulders, and your seat on your bike as you ride. Feel the paintbrush in your hand as you move colour over the canvas or the water pressure against your arms, and the rhythm of your breath, as you swim. Bring your attention fully to your body and tune in to the precision of your movement and the rhythm of your breath whatever activity you are doing. Acknowledge any feelings of tension and see if you can also find freedom in your body and mind. So if you notice feelings of frustration, can find satisfaction as well? Observe yourself having these experiences rather than allowing them to hook your attention.

Appendix 4

The Spiritual Aspect – Finding Deeper Connection

As we've journeyed together through this book, we've talked about backpacks full of memories and beliefs and roads that get narrowed and horizons dimmed because of our doubts and fears. We've discussed the need for intellectual, emotional, physical, and spiritual well-being. We've explored the intricate link between these aspects of ourselves; and we've discovered that when healthy and in balance they will propel us with clarity, confidence, energy, and inspiration towards our potential. We've talked about how to *pay attention* to our thoughts, *embrace* our emotions, and *explore* our feelings, and how this internal inquiry with a generous sprinkling of self-compassion, will win out over forced external motivation every time. We've reacquainted ourselves with the feeling of pure potential and realised the power of the mind, that can bring us to our knees, literally, if we're not managing it well. So where does the spiritual aspect fit into all this and how do we experience it?

I ran some workshops recently and asked the participants to tell me how they felt when they were in touch with spirit or enjoying health in the spiritual aspect of themselves. Here are some of the words they came up with that describe this healthy spiritual state.

Calm, connected, grounded, composed, peaceful, kind, loving, accepting, creative, flowing, still, grateful, inspired, trusting, balanced, full, strong, compassionate, purposeful, intuitive, dedicated, oneness and potential. All these words, and I'm sure many more, describe what is experienced when we become acquainted with the spiritual aspect of ourselves.

The Buddha taught that emptiness is one's true nature, and that through this emptiness the Divine states of compassion, loving-kindness, empathetic joy, and equanimity are achieved. It would certainly seem that my friends in the workshop agree and that they have at times experienced this state of Being. This aspect of you is unchanging and is always available to you beneath your conditioned thoughts, beliefs, and blocks that cause distortion. In my experience, our spiritual aspect offers a deep sense of peace, trust, unconditional love, connection, and with that, genuine control.

I often find that during meditation I have highly creative ideas and I write these ideas down as this "inspired" conversation emerges. This is the third type of conversation I alluded to earlier in the book. Albert Einstein said, "I think ninety-nine times and find nothing. I stop thinking, swim in silence, and the truth comes to me." What he's alluding to is the profound creativity and awareness that emerges when we experience silence. Not that I'm comparing myself to Albert!

I began this book by describing how the bulb inside an onion is like the bulb of potential you were born as, and how the layers around the bulb are like the layers of conditioning that happen as you grow up, smothering the bulb. That bulb of pure potential emerges through practicing the exercises in this book. As you slowly peel away the layers of conditioning, you'll get to know your true nature, and spend more time living from that part of yourself. All the practices in this book will guide you on a journey to your true nature, a state you've already experienced at times in your life.

Let's think about that for a moment. Imagine if you were to live from the part of yourself that knows compassion, loving-kindness, empathetic joy, and equanimity, meaning you feel compassion for yourself and others, you feel loving-kindness for yourself and others, you can delight in your own and another's good fortune, and enjoy a sense of balance within yourself and life. Imagine the positive reach this would have for you and your life! True nature is revealed through the expression of your unique self as you move towards your potential with more acceptance, confidence, and inspiration.

When you sit in meditation you can *embrace* and *explore* your thoughts, emotions, and feelings by simply letting them be present. You realise you can observe your thoughts, emotions, and feelings just as you would observe your breath or your next-door neighbour's cat! As you become more and more familiar with taking the stance of the observer, rather than being embroiled, you'll start to experience the emptiness the Buddha described. It's in this emptiness that you'll realise you are not your thoughts, emotions, or feelings; they are simply things that are happening to you, but they do not define you. And if you allow yourself the comfort of visiting this empty place often, you'll *connect* to your true nature.

Dedicated Practice – True Nature Meditation

- **Use this to help you Connect with and Express your Unique Potential**

I'm going to leave you with one more meditation, a meditation I hope will help bring you home to your true nature and enable you to express your unique pure potential in whatever way feels right for you in your life.

As with the previous practices, it would be valuable to record these meditation instructions or get a friend or family member to read them to you. Remember you can also download the free audio recording by using the QR code at the back of the book or going to: www.rutholiver.com.au/recordings

Exercise 15 – True Nature Meditation

You'll notice, as you concentrate on your body in this meditation, that the natural relaxation response your body produces when you give it attention will take place. Enjoy dropping into this focussed, still, and relaxed state of observation. This is where not only will your physical body rest and regenerate, but you become more deeply acquainted with your true nature.

Find a comfortable, quiet place to sit. Move your hips into the back of the seat so your back is supported by the chair. You want your body to be comfortable but upright. Of course, if you can't sit, please lie down for this meditation. Settle your body and ensure that you feel extremely comfortable.

Bring your attention to all the sensory information that's coming to you. And as you settle into this supposedly quiet time, notice there's quite a lot going on.

Sound ... taste ... smell ... sensation ... and of course, thoughts. Let this very natural process of picking up sensory information happen without trying to stop it. (*Pause.*)

Gradually begin to bring your attention to the building where you are. Or if you're outside, to the surrounding area. (*Pause.*)

Now bring your attention to where you're sitting or lying down. (*Pause.*) And then bring your attention to your body. (*Pause.*) Become very conscious of your whole body. (*Pause*).

Notice that sensory information comes to you as feelings and sensations, images, thoughts, or things you hear. (*Pause.*) Simply *pay attention* to the activity of the mind. And begin to e*mbrace* all this activity as if you were embracing a small child that wants your attention and you say, "It's okay, just sit quietly next to me, I'm going to be focusing on something else for a while." (*Pause.*)

Now start to bring your attention to your breath, following your breath as you breathe in and being very aware of your body as you breathe out. (*Pause.*) Let your breath be gentle and natural with no effort to change it. (*Pause.*) Occasionally you may get the urge to take a deep breath and let out a sigh.

Bring your attention to your seat. To your hips and sit bones and the whole pelvic bowl. Rest here a while embracing and exploring the seat of your body. (*Pause.*) Follow your inhale with deep attention and as you exhale take your focus to your seat and allow yourself to feel grounded. (*Long Pause.*)

In your own time move your attention to your spine. Notice this part of your body that helps hold you upright. Rest here, while observing the length and lift of your spine. (*Pause.*) Notice when your mind wanders, and continually coax your attention back to your breath and your spine. Breathe in with a clear focus on your breath and as you exhale place your attention on the lift of your spine feeling stable. (*Long pause.)*

Now move your attention to your shoulders. *Embrace* and *explore* all sensations in your shoulders. (*Pause.)* Engage fully with your breath, as you exhale let your attention fall to your shoulders, and allow yourself to feel relaxed. (*Long pause.)*

Gently take your attention to the crown of your head. *Embrace* and *explore* all feelings and sensations at your crown. (*Pause.)* As you breathe in, be fully present with your breath and as you exhale let your attention rest at your crown. Allow yourself to feel a sense of your connection to everything. (*Long pause.)*

Draw your attention to your face, in particular noticing your forehead, eyes, mouth, and your jaw. (*Pause.)* Stay here a while and *embrace* and *explore* all feelings and sensations in your face, and as you exhale enjoy a feeling of peace wash over you. (*Long Pause.)*

Now, drop your attention to your heart and rest here a while, *embracing* and *exploring* the different feelings and sensations that appear. (*Pause.)* If your mind becomes distracted that's okay. Simply remind it that you're not engaging in a conversation now but choosing to have your attention rest at your heart centre. Breathe out and allow yourself to be immersed in feelings of loving-kindness and compassion. (*Long pause.)*

And now let your attention gently move to your breath. Let your breath be like an incredibly soft caress as it moves effortlessly in and out of your body. (*Pause.)* Take your time to acquaint yourself with your breath. Notice how it moves your body. Notice as you get to the top of your inhale the moment your breath turns around and becomes an exhale. (*Pause.*) Then watch as you reach the end of your exhale the moment the breath turns around and becomes an inhale. (*Pause.*) Effortless, easy breathing. Stay here a while, enjoying your breath. (*Long pause.)*

Then can you let your focus of attention move away from being engrossed in the feelings and sensations and movements of your breath and watch your breath from the standpoint of an observer? So, you are no longer in the movie of breath, you are now just watching the movie. Rest here a while simply observing your breath. (*Long pause.*) Notice how your mind becomes still and you sometimes drop into what Buddha called emptiness. Your true nature. *(Pause).* Take your time. (*Long pause.*)

And again, rotate your attention through the points of connection in your body. Seat … *(Long pause).* Spine … *(Long pause).* Shoulders … *(Long pause).* Crown … *(Long pause).* Face … *(Long pause).* Heart … *(Long pause).* Back to the breath. *(Long pause).* Take your time, rest in stillness as you simply observe your breath. (*Long Pause.*)

Notice how you can be the observer of all sensory information that comes across your path. Simply watch rather than engaging with this information. (*Long pause.*)

Recall those innocent moments you had as a child of complete trust and wonder and allow yourself to drop into this childlike state with a feeling that everything is ok in your world. (*Pause.*) Stay here until you sense you've found within you a deep sense of safety, ease, and love. (*Pause.*)

Simply watch and notice that under all stimuli that come through our senses there's a still, quiet place that feels like home. (*Pause.*) This place is always there waiting for you to arrive. It's your true nature from where you can access your full potential. (*Pause.*)

Stay in your meditation as long as you like reminding yourself of the seven points of connection if your mind becomes distracted. Seat … spine … shoulders … crown … face … heart … and back to the breath… And into stillness.

Connect in Daily Life

You will already have activities in your life where you are in touch with your spiritual nature, they're the things that give you endless pleasure, the activities you get so absorbed in that time becomes irrelevant. Maybe you're an avid gardener and love being out in nature and this brings you a sense of connection with yourself and the world. Perhaps you're an artist and love to express yourself through your music or craft. Or you might love to dance or engage in a physical activity that makes you feel alive and vibrant. Ask yourself what you enjoy, and then ask yourself why you don't engage in these activities more often. (This could be a good question for a Stream of Consciousness writing session…)

I love to paint, but even though I love it, I sometimes put it off because my mind tells me I have more important things to do. Somewhere in my unconscious, there's a habitual message that tells me not to waste my time painting. And yet, when I do it, I feel satisfied and connected to myself in ways I never do when I'm doing so-called "important" things. Over the years, I've learned to *pay attention* to the voice that tells me not to get my paints out. I've discovered how to *embrace* and *explore* the resistance my mind throws up and come home to my true nature that will always guide me in the right direction. Usually, I end up having a wonderful day of painting!

Often the things we love to do get sidelined because of our busy lives, so ensure that you schedule weekly time to *connect* with your true nature through the things you enjoy and the ways you express yourself. In this way, you'll *connect* with and express your authentic self in your life.

I'll leave you with one of my favourite quotes. It's a reminder that the quiet space we find when we attend to our thoughts, feelings, and emotions and access our true nature, is where we'll find a response to life's challenges. It takes me back to childhood moments on that silent hillside in the Lake District, where I would experience freedom and pure potential.

As an adult, you'll access these moments more as you nurture your well-being by practicing the meditations and other exercises shown here. You'll feel reassured that butterflies are normal, nothing to be feared, simply a shared human experience; urging you to come home to the space where stillness, response, and freedom lie. This is where you'll access your greatest potential and shine in your life.

> "Between stimulus and response there is a space.
> In that space is our power to choose our response.
> In our response lies our growth and our freedom."
>
> *Viktor Frankl*

Appendix 5

A Summary of the Exercises in this book and How to Use Them

Chapter 3 - The Narrow Road
Exercise 1 – Tuning into Feeling
This visualisation is important to do periodically as it will remind you of how you want to feel in your life. It's useful to do when you want to reassess or remind yourself of your values and motivations so you can be more intentional about the way you live and enjoy more success.

Chapter 8 - The Four Aspects
Exercise 2 - The 4 Aspects Health Check
Use this written exercise to map out which areas of your life you'd like to improve. Don't wait until your life is in turmoil or drift through life hoping for the best. Identify now where you could enjoy more potential, success, and happiness so you feel inspired to learn and grow.

Chapter 14 - Step 1: Pay Attention – Airing out the Intellectual Aspect
Exercise 3 - Thought Cascade
When faced with a difficult situation use this written exercise to uncover your unconscious thoughts, feelings, and emotions. This will help you understand the depth of your reactive mind which is a very cleansing process.

Chapter 15 - Step 2: Embrace and Explore – Airing out the Emotional and Physical Aspect
Exercise 4 – Tuning in to Thoughts, Emotions, and Sensations
This exercise will help you see how your thoughts trigger emotions and elicit a physical response in the body. Practicing this will help you be more comfortable with uncomfortable thoughts, emotions, and feelings, so you become adept at living with a range of emotions and feelings in daily life.

Chapter 16 – Step 3: Connect – Airing out the Spiritual Aspect
Exercise 5 – Simple Meditation
Enjoy this simple meditation to practice relaxing your body and calming your mind. This is a good meditation to do first thing in the morning, even before you get out of bed. It will help you start the day with a peaceful demeanour and a clear mind.

APPENDICES
1 - Doing the Inner Work
Exercise 6 - The Four Aspects Health Check
This written exercise will help you identify what feels healthy and unhealthy in the intellectual, emotional, physical, and spiritual aspects of you. By doing this you will understand yourself at a deeper level and be alert to finding balance.

2 – The Intellectual Aspect – Overcoming Monotonous Conversation and Mind Chatter
Exercise 7 – The Conscious Inventory
A good calming alternative to meditation, this writing exercise will help you be more conscious and clear a busy mind. As long as you have a pen and paper you can do this any time to help restore mindful focus and relaxation.

Exercise 8 – Stream of Consciousness Writing
A wonderful way to start the day, this exercise helps you access unconscious mind chatter. Sometimes this mind chatter is useful, and you'll have insights and great ideas. At other times it's helpful to clear it from your mind. Writing in this way will help you work through an issue or make sense of something that's upsetting you. It's also a very good way of putting your thoughts in order and can be very therapeutic. It can also be a good way to brainstorm. The key is to let your writing flow and see where it takes you. Doing this exercise is a good prelude to your meditation because once your thoughts are on paper the mind can relax, and you'll enjoy your meditation more.

3 – The Emotional and Physical Aspect – Living Comfortably with Emotions and Feelings.
Exercise 9 – Breath and Body Meditation
This meditation builds on the Simple Meditation in chapter 16. When you practice embracing and exploring all emotions and feelings in meditation, your nervous system will feel soothed, and you'll feel more relaxed. Practicing this in meditation will help you to access this healthy state of mind and body in your everyday life, which will enable you to respond to life's challenges rather than react.

Exercise 10 – Breath and Body Meditation as you go about your day
You can practice this Breath and Body Meditation anytime, anywhere, because you don't have to close your eyes. This is to prompt you to be more conscious and focussed at times when you may normally let your mind roam. Instead, focus on the task at hand, your breath, and your body as you engage in your daily activities.

Exercise 11 – Daily Activities to Hone the Mind
A reminder of daily activities that happen often where you can practice mindful living. Doing this helps you gain control of a wandering mind that might cause anxiety.

Exercise 12 – Balance the Scales Meditation
This meditation is based on the ancient practice of yoga nidra or yogic sleep. It will not only facilitate a natural state of deep relaxation but will help you explore opposites of emotions and feelings in the body. Being aware of the myriad of emotions and feelings available to you will help you navigate challenges in your life with more acceptance and composure.

Exercise 13 – Mountain Pose
Mountain pose is a simple foundational yoga posture and ignites a physical and energetic sense of grounded, empowered control. It's not only powerful but relaxing as well because standing in this way brings alignment and support to your body. It will enable you to tune into the present moment more dynamically. It's a great posture to stand in for a few moments after your meditation or any time during your day when you might normally fall into bad posture.

Exercise 14 – Finding the Zone
Finding the Zone is a reminder to access your potential and enjoy effortless action by learning to embrace whatever experience you have as you take part in exercise and activity.

4 – The Spiritual Aspect – Finding Deeper Connection
Exercise 15 – True Nature Meditation
This meditation will enable you to access deep relaxation and help you become the observer of the sensory information that comes your way, rather than engaging with it. When you practice regularly with patience and persistence, you'll access your true nature of compassion, loving-kindness, equanimity, and joy, the place of pure potential.

Further Resources

Thank you for joining me on this journey, I hope you've gained value from reading my book, but most of all I hope that you'll continue this journey to greater self-awareness. Keep reading, keep meditating, keep learning and growing, and never doubt that you can overcome obstacles in your life and find success and happiness.

If you'd like access to more of my resources to help you implement simple daily practices, or give you techniques to manage the bigger challenges in life; as well as information on how to make the daily 'edits' needed to keep you on an upward spiral of well-being and potential - here are some places you can go.

For access to free audio recordings of the meditations in this book, go to www.rutholiver.com.au/recordings or scan this QR code.

Scan Me

To learn more about my programs and to sign up for my newsletter - which only comes out a couple of times a month and is full of juicy information, visit: www.rutholiver.com.au

And if you'd like to join my Facebook group, which is specifically to help women take care of their well-being and unlock their full potential go to: https://www.facebook.com/groups/wisewomanproject

About the Author

Ruth Oliver is a sought-after speaker, group facilitator, and coach on well-being and potential. She is the founder of The Oliver Method a simple tool that enables people to understand the power of mind-body well-being and move beyond its limitations.

Beginning her journey into well-being many years ago as a fitness instructor, she quickly realised through some life-changing events, that to unlock more potential and be successful one must address the health of mind and body.

Ruth works with individuals and groups both publicly and in the corporate sector. She facilitates programs online, and in-person, as well as weekend intensives and retreats. She brings her knowledge and tools to people (particularly women) who are wanting to manage everyday stress and feel more capable and confident, so they can unlock their full potential and enjoy more happiness and success in life.

Ruth grew up in England and now lives in Melbourne, Australia with her husband. Alongside her well-being programs, she teaches yoga and Pilates. In her spare time, you'll find her on the river training (as well as having lots of laughs) with her rowing buddies. She loves nothing more than spending time with her family or getting on a plane and embarking on new adventures.

Acknowledgments

First and foremost, I want to thank the many people who over the years have asked me for help and trusted me when they were at their most vulnerable. To all those who have attended my programs, come to my weekly classes, or had coaching from me, thank you. Your support of my work inspires me to continue learning and become better at what I do.

Thank you, Tom Bird for your unique and inspiring guidance that enabled me to put the first words of this book down on the page in such a spontaneous and natural way. Butterflies are Normal would not have happened without you. And to the staff at Jetlaunch who have been so patient and caring throughout the editing and design process.

To Kathy Morton Stanion for allowing me to grace the cover of my book with your beautiful butterfly artwork, thank you! Your excitement about this creative project has been heart-warming. To see more of Kathy's work, go to - https://www.artfinder.com/artist/kathy-morton-stanion/#/

A heartfelt thank you also goes to my dear friends Lisa Ceruto and Debbie Williams who lovingly enhanced my writing and gave me lots of encouragement. And to Charli Fels at Ostrich 180 Publishing who gently guided me over the finish line.

My deepest gratitude to Dr. Richard Miller, founder of the iRest Institute. I feel privileged to have you as my teacher.

My thanks and love to my husband Mark. I'm a lucky lady to live with someone who understands the importance of having meaning and purpose in life and gives me endless support in the pursuit of mine.

And to you! Thank you for coming on this journey with me. I hope we meet again as you continue to show up and shine in your life.

Manufactured by Amazon.com.au
Sydney, New South Wales, Australia

13273564R00108